HISTORY OF
MACK TRUCKS

D1604750

Tom Brownell

Motorbooks International
Publishers & Wholesalers ®

First published in 1994 by Motorbooks International
Publishers & Wholesalers, PO Box 2, 729 Prospect Avenue,
Osceola, WI 54020 USA

Motorbooks International is a certified trademark,
registered with the United States Patent Office

The information in this book is true and complete to the
best of our knowledge. All recommendations are made
without any guarantee on the part of the author or
Publisher, who also disclaim any liability incurred in
connection with the use of this data or specific details

We recognize that some words, model names and
designations, for example, mentioned herein are the
property of the trademark holder. We use them for
identification purposes only. This is not an official
publication

Motorbooks International books are also available at
discounts in bulk quantity for industrial or sales-
promotional use. For details write to Special Sales
Manager at the Publisher's address

Library of Congress Cataloging-in-Publication Data

Brownell, Tom.
    History of Mack Trucks/Tom Brownell.
        p. cm.
    Includes index.
    ISBN 0-87938-946-X
    1. Mack Trucks—History. I. Title.
TL230.5.M17B76   1994
629.224—dc20   94-32973

On the front cover: This stunning B-77 is no show horse.
It's still a working truck based in Idaho. *Stan Holtzman/
Line Rigs*

On the back cover: Bruce Thomas' LT logging truck, *Stan
Holtzman/Line Rigs;* an MB model, which was a strictly
functional truck with its tall cab, immense windshield, and
set-back axle; and modern Mack trucks, which continue
the company's spirit of excellence. *Tom Brownell*

Printed and bound in the United States

Contents

Introduction

Mack Trucks —
As American as Apple Pie

When I hear the name Mack, I see myself standing in the loading door of a dairy. It's the summer between my sophomore and junior years at college. I'm swinging crates filled with gallon jugs of milk onto a roller rack that disappears behind a canvas curtain into the cavernous cargo bay of a truck that seems ancient to me. The managers of that dairy ran a "get by" operation, and rather than invest in a cooler of adequate size to hold the dairy products for a day's distribution, they purchased a refrigerator-bodied Mack that had been retired from highway service. From my vantage point in the late 1950s, I thought the refrigerator truck to be a 1920s model. Actually it was a mid-'30s B model Mack. I never knew the truck to leave the dairy's lot, but it would start. On at least a couple of occasions, another summer hire and I fired the old Mack up and exercised it in the parking lot. It was a lumbering beast, but what a sense of "king of the road" we got as we took turns manhandling the controls.

Years later, while doing research for this book, I discovered that that B Series Mack I'd loaded milk into at the dairy still existed, though stripped of its refrigerator body. Seems that a local collector by the name of Grover Swank had made the dairy owners an offer they couldn't refuse and had purchased the beast for its value as scrap. As we walked around the dairy truck's chassis, Grover advised, "It's got a bad clutch, guess you know that, but it still runs. I took the body off because it was rotted. Fix the clutch, put on a good cab and straight body, and this would be one fine-running, impressive truck." Grover was right. Stripped to its bones it exuded Mack brawn, the stuff from which legends—in this case the Mack legend—is born.

Visiting Grover Swank's collection and climbing over his trucks helped me get a firsthand feel for his-

toric Macks. But to put together a book on these trucks I needed data, and Mack literature is about as easy to come by as a "good morning, how are you" in downtown Manhattan. This being the case, I am extremely grateful to Colin Chisholm, curator of the Mack Museum, for giving me access to the museum's files. Practically every stick of Mack literature ever printed resides in the Mack Museum's fireproof file drawers. And what isn't explained in the literature, Colin knows from his vast, lifelong experience with Mack trucks. When I explained to Colin the frustration I was experiencing trying to understand how Mack categorized and identified its engines, Colin unrolled a six-foot scroll on which he had drawn a time line with the identifying nomenclature of each engine and the date it was introduced. The scroll didn't make all the numbers as clear as a toot from an air horn, but it helped me feel better about my confusion.

A book of this sort needs pictures; and while I'd found myself having a photographer's field day with the Mack showing at the Antique Truck Club of America's Annual Father's Day Weekend gathering in Macungie, Pennsylvania, it's never possible to find all models of any make of truck at one event. So that the widest range of models could be represented, Hope Emerick—editor of *Double Clutch*, the publication of the Antique Truck Club of America—made her collection of Mack photos available. Colin Chisholm and the Mack Museum have also been helpful in providing Mack factory photographs.

Whether you're a Mack owner or admirer, it's my hope that this book will give you a better understanding and appreciation for the trucks that collectively have created the legend "Built Like a Mack Truck."

Chapter 1

"Built Like a Mack Truck": How the Legend Began

The Mack legend traces its origin to the dawn of this century when, following several years building wagons and experimenting with self-propelled vehicles, five brothers with the family name of Mack constructed and sold their first commercial vehicle in 1901. No, that first Mack wasn't a truck—it was a bus.

Why a bus? It seems that Augustus ("Gus") Mack had been treated to a ride in a Winton touring car—an experience that created a life-changing impression. But rather than attempt to build a vehicle that would compete with Winton, the Macks decided to target what today would be called a "market niche," which is a small but preexisting demand for a particular type of vehicle. The market they saw was for a self-propelled sightseeing bus. Not by coincidence, the first Mack bus closely resembled the Winton touring car on an expanded scale with 36in diameter tires and 4in rubber tires. From the start the Mack brothers focused upon what would become the key ingredient to the company's success: premium quality construction. The axles of that first bus were constructed of high-grade nickel steel and the chassis had at least a 2,000lb capacity.

The Macks built the bus's four-cylinder engine to their own innovative design. The engine carried a hefty power rating of 36hp, which was several times the power output of the gasoline engines found in cars of the day. The chassis held a tonneau-style body with seating capacity of 15 passengers. Actually the passenger capacity of early Mack buses is in some dispute since the seats were wide enough to fit four abreast allowing a full passenger load of 18 to 20. This first bus saw successful operation in Prospect Park, New York, and—as with any good product—soon led to an order for a second bus from the same customer. That second sale, placed in 1903, apparently convinced the Macks that they were in the bus business to stay and an advertising campaign was launched to bring in new customers.

At first each bus was custom-built, allowing the product to be tailored to the needs of the customer. Even before their bus designs had stabilized, the Mack brothers were thinking in other directions. As early as 1904, John ("Jack") and Gus Mack were experimenting with a 90hp engine. Like some other early manufacturers, Henry Ford to name a notable example, the Macks weren't "playing" with horsepower to win races or set speed records. Rather they sought horsepower to move loads, and the bigger the load the more power needed.

The 1907 seven-seat, 27-passenger bus on display at the Mack Museum. This bus is built on a Mack Sr. chassis and therefore features right-hand drive. One of the rather odd characteristics of the early Macks is that all Mack Sr. trucks used right-hand drive while the Mack Jr. trucks used left-hand drive.

A 1911 Mack Jr. 1-1/12 ton truck on display at the Mack Museum. This truck's four-cylinder engine produced 32hp, quite a respectable figure for the day. Note the left-hand drive.

The first Mack trucks were delivery-style models built on the bus chassis. These trucks were powered by a 50hp engine and featured a patented constant-mesh, selective-gear transmission.

Because the Macks referred to their buses as motor cars, they called their company the Mack Bros. Motor Car Company—Mack Trucks Inc. wouldn't appear for nearly 20 years and only after the Macks had left the enterprise that made their name world famous. In 1905, the Macks moved their bus-building operation from New York to Allentown, Pennsylvania. Sales increased; by the end of that year the total number of buses built reached 51, and the product line had expanded to include trucks. The first Mack trucks were two delivery-style models built on the bus chassis and rated at 1-1/2 and 2 tons, plus a 5-ton model for heavy use. Power for the new trucks came from a new 50hp engine with a 5.5in bore and 6in stroke. This engine remained in production through 1915. In addition to premium quality materials and a proprietary engine, these early trucks also featured advanced (for their time) engineering, being fitted with a patented constant-mesh selective gear transmission. All three qualities, premium materials,

"MACK," TYPE ONE, with Dust Proof Van Body.
Four in service.

Mack Hi-Cab Van 1905-1915

Mack pioneered cab-over-engine trucks with this early Hi-Cab Van of 1905-1915.

proprietary engines, and advanced engineering foreshadowed those characteristics that would give substance to the "Built like a Mack truck" legend.

So popular were the new motor buses and trucks that the Mack operation at Allentown had swelled to 700 employees by 1911. Another 50 men were employed in Brooklyn and an additional 75 worked in a newly acquired engine plant in Newark, New Jersey. Almost overnight Mack had become one of largest builders of heavy-duty motor trucks with more than 3 tons of capacity). The company's adver-

tising emphasized Mack's success, boasting the "Leading Gasoline Truck of America."

Mack Bros. Motor Car Co. was beginning to feel the effects of too much of a good thing, however. Production for 1911 hit a high of 600 buses and trucks, but with the record output came a need for expansion capital. In October 1911, the Mack brothers combined their interests with the newly formed Sauer Motor Co., which held a license to build Swiss-designed Sauer trucks in America. Rather than a merger, the two companies continued separate manufacturing operations under a financial holding company called the International Motor Company (IMC). Sales and service, however, were combined. The Sauer was a quality truck with load ratings similar to the larger Mack models; bringing together the sales operations of two nose-to-nose competitors may not have been the best idea.

In 1913, IMC added a third truck line, these being the trucks built by the Hewitt Motor Co. of New York City. The combination of Mack, Sauer, and Hewitt gave, as the IMC's ads proclaimed, "A truck for every need of every industry." Now the lineup ranged from the 1-ton Mack Jr. to a 10-ton Hewitt. But more important than a wider product range, in acquiring Hewitt Motor Co., International also gained the engineering talents of two men whose genius would make Mack the preeminent truck builder. Edward R. Hewitt, founder of the company that bore his name, would serve for 30 years as Mack's chief engineer and have as the crowning achievement of his talents the AB (built from 1914 to 1936). Another brilliant engineer, Alfred F. Masury would design the AC "Bulldog" Mack—one of the most famous trucks ever built. From Masury, too, would come the Bulldog hood ornament found on every Mack since 1932. As the International Motor Company's directors were predominantly bankers, they may have missed the human treasure contained in the Hewitt purchase.

Just when its future looked brightest, International Motor Company's fortunes took a precipitous fall. In 1913, sales fell 30 percent, not from a lack of a wide range of quality products, but due to increased competition by new entries into the motor truck field (particularly from car makers such as Packard and General Motors). To survive, IMC needed a cash infusion that could only come from outside investors.

In the midst of this financial turbulence and prospects of diminished control of the company they had founded, Joe and Jack left International Motor Company's board. While the men themselves would be lost to history and settle into oblivion, the trucks that bore the Mack name would go on to build an illustrious history. After failing in another truck-building venture, Jack Mack operated an agency selling Republic trucks. This founding figure in the Mack truck legend died tragically on March 24, 1924, while on a business trip when the car he was driving was struck by a trolley. Appropriately, his grave marker in Allentown, Pennsylvania's Fairview Cemetery reads, "Jack M. Mack, 1865-1924, Founder of Mack Truck."

By 1916, the greatly increased demand for motor trucks, resulting in part from orders for trucks to ply the blood-soaked fields of France, but also from greater reliance on heavy trucks to move goods at home, led to the formation of a new holding company called International Motor Truck Corp., which absorbed International Motor Company. Under the reorganization, the Hewitt name was dropped, showing management's recognition of the redundancy in truck models, but also reflecting the sales success of the recently introduced Mack AB line.

In 1919, Sauer likewise disappeared, leaving Mack as International Motor Truck Corp.'s sole product name. Afterwards, the idea of the parent company and its chief product wearing different names seemed more than inconsistent. It led to confusion and recognition problems between International Motor Truck Co. and International Harvester, which built International trucks. It came as little surprise, then, that on March 22, 1922, International Motor Truck Corp.'s directors voted to change the company name to Mack Trucks Inc. With its corporate and product identity firmly established, Mack trucks began building a reputation unmatched by any other truck manufacturer worldwide.

Chapter 2

Mack AB Series

As the first new truck designed by the International Motor Company, the AB represents the original or oldest "Mack." In 1914, the newly formed International Motor Company set up its corporate headquarters in a new building in New York City and immediately enlisted the talents of Edward R. Hewitt, who had been named chief engineer, to design a new medium-duty truck to replace the Mack Jr. In less than a year, Hewitt and his staff had not only completed their design work, but the truck itself was actually in production. As a light- to medium-duty model, early ABs were built with load ratings of 1, 1-1/2, and 2 tons. The 1-ton would be dropped in 1918 and eventually models rated up to 10 tons would be offered.

The AB pioneered design principles that would appear a few years later on the heavier-duty AC model and would mark the "signature" of Mack Trucks, giving Mack its legendary reputation for ruggedness and reliability. Key to the AB's design was what can best be described as "straightforward simplicity." Without frills and needless complexities, E. R. Hewitt and his team had designed a truck that did the job expected of it. The formula was simple: combine superior strength alloy steels and drop forging, oversized bearings and shafts, extra-wide gears, and close accuracy in workmanship to create a product that would give long service with minimal care. The slogan "Built like a Mack Truck" hadn't been

The AB pioneered design principles that would appear a few years later in the heavier AC model and would mark the "signature" of Mack trucks, giving Mack its legendary reputation for ruggedness and reliability. Early ABs, such as the 1914-1936-style depicted here, are distinguished by hard rubber tires and a smaller radiator that matches the height of the hood.

coined yet, but with the AB the substance for the slogan had been put in place.

Although the basic features of the AB's four-cylinder engine varied little from other engine designs of its day, Hewitt and his staff gave special attention to areas that would help ensure long engine life. For example, three unusually large 3in-diameter main journals prevented the crankshaft from whipping and flexing. The crankpin journals, likewise, measured a healthy 2-1/4in in diameter. To assure machining precision, the cylinders, measuring 4-1/2x5in, were cast in-block, then annealed and rebored. For ease of service, the heads were detachable and cast in pairs. Placing the valves in the block simplified the valve mechanism.

A thoughtful feature that would also appear on the AC, the crankcase casting contained large inspection ports that enabled mechanics to inspect the condition of the crankshaft and connecting rod bearings without disassembling the engine. Since the condition of the lubricating oil plays a major factor in prolonging or shortening the life of an engine, care was taken to incorporate a double screen oil filtering system. Also, water from the engine's cooling system circulated around the oil reservoir in the front of the block features to bring the oil quickly up to operating temperatures for cold weather operation and to keep the oil cool in hot weather conditions.

Originally, Mack rated the AB's engine at 30hp. Later sales literature shows a 60hp rating. A centrifu-

Mack AB Road Oiler 1914-1936

Mack introduced its famous dual reduction axle on the AB Series in 1920 as a replacement for worm gear rear drive. As the name implies, the dual reduction axle contains two sets of gears: a pinion gear, similar to what might be found inside the rear axle of any modern day car or truck, and a larger bull gear which turns the axle shafts. This

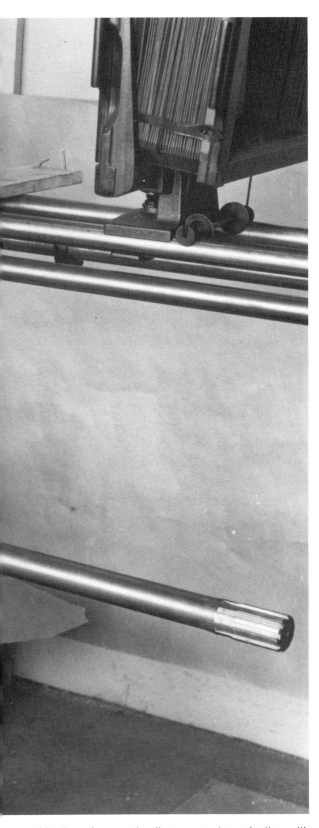

combination of gear sets allows a greater reduction with significantly less torque stress on the gears.
Mack Museum

gal governor limited road speed to 16mph. Hard rubber tires used on early trucks necessitated speed control to prevent the truck from being hammered to pieces by the constant jarring forces transmitted to the chassis by the solid tires. The AB used three methods for transferring power to the rear wheels. Trucks built in 1914 were fitted with Timken worm drives. In 1915, chain drive also became available. In 1921, Mack introduced a novel and patented Hotchkiss-style "dual-reduction" rear axle that incorporated great strength with increased road clearance. Early AB models used a fairly large number of purchased parts, including Brown-Lipe three-speed transmissions. Later, as Mack brought more of its part manufacturing in-house, the gear box was upgraded to a four-speed unit. Shifting was accomplished by means of a dry multiple disk clutch.

Although the AB's mechanical design progressed through numerous changes over the model's life, its styling remained quite static, changing dramatically only once. The AB's appearance didn't make a special statement, as would be the case with the "Bull Dog" AC. Rather, the narrow cowl, forward-sloping hood, and front-mounted radiator gave the new "Baby Mack" line a pleasantly up-to-date look in 1914. By the early 1920s, AB Macks were being fitted with pneumatic tires, which not only changed the truck's appearance somewhat but gave a vastly improved ride and allowed greater speeds. The first real styling change occurred in 1923 when a larger radiator using fin-and-tube construction replaced the original cellular-construction radiator. Since the larger radiator stood a little taller than the front edge of the cowl, the hood would have had to slope "uphill" to mate with the new radiator's contours. Obviously, an uphill hood would give the truck a somewhat ridiculous look, so the hood stamping was redesigned slightly to allow the hood to extend almost horizontal from the cowl, leaving the radiator standing slightly higher than the hood. Actually, the larger radiator improved the truck's looks, giving it a stronger, more rugged appearance.

Although Mack introduced a new light-duty line called the BB model in 1928, the AB continued in production through the mid-1930s. Finally, in 1933, the AB shed its 1914-era styling that looked almost antique and adopted the fully enclosed cab and sharply squared-off lines, along with the heavier fenders and more massive radiator of the B Series trucks. Mack can never be accused of making changes for change's sake. All modifications to the original AB design occurred as improvements became available and to offer owners increased service and comfort—never simply for the sake of novelty.

Probably the AB Mack's most exceptional feature was the dual reduction axle introduced in 1920 as a replacement for the worm gear rear drive, which had been the alternative to chain drive since 1915. (Even after the introduction of the dual reduction rear axle, chain drive continued as an alternative for buyers who wanted that mechanism's exceptional ruggedness and durability.) Mack's patented dual reduction drive offered several unique design characteristics that set it apart from other drive mechanisms. For those who get an opportunity to crawl under the rear of an AB Mack equipped with a dual reduction axle, probably the design quirk noticed first is the angle of the differential housing. Typically, the rear axle banjo (the large oval casting holding the rear end gears) inclined away from the axle, rather than face perpendicular to the axle. Mack engineers put the axle gear case at an oblique angle to help the casting absorb road shocks, which their tests showed normally occurred in an oblique direction. Placing the casting in the same direction as the road shocks made for a much stronger rear axle housing and a much smaller chance of breaking this essential structure.

The second design structure that an under-truck examination is likely to show is the gear casing that extends forward from the axle banjo. If one didn't know an AB Mack's construction, one might think these trucks featured a transaxle, the combination of transmission and rear axle in one unit. However, as has already been discussed, this isn't the case with the AB, which mounts its transmission in the orthodox location directly behind the engine. The question then becomes: what's the purpose of the gear casing attached to the rear axle?

Actually, the dual reduction axle, as its name implies, contains two sets of gears. Attached to the end of the driveshaft, as it enters the dual reduction axle's gear casing, is a pinion gear, similar to what might be found inside the rear axle of any modern car or truck. As is common practice, this pinion gear engages a ring gear, which transfers the engine's rearward rotational forces to lateral rotation for driving the wheels. However, the ring gear does not also turn the axle shafts as is the situation in most rear axles. Instead, attached to the ring gear is a smaller drive gear that runs against a larger bull gear, which rotates inside the axle banjo. The bull gear turns the axle shafts. This combination of gear sets gives the dual reduction axle its name.

For those who get an opportunity to view a dual reduction axle, probably the feature that will be noticed first is the angle of the differential housing. Mack engineers put the gear casing at an oblique angle to help the casting absorb road shocks. A second unusual design feature is the gear housing which extends forward from the casting. This housing contains the pinion gearset. Mack Museum

The AB underwent its first real styling change in 1923 when a larger radiator using fin-and-tube construction replaced the original cellular-construction radiator. Since the larger radiator stood a little taller than the front edge of the cowl, the hood would have had to slope up to mate with the new radiator's contours. The simple solution was

The first AB models were fitted with Timken worm drives; chain drive became available in 1915. This 1922 AB 2-1/2 ton chain-drive truck is on permanent display at the Mack museum.

to have the radiator stand taller than the front of the hood, an easy recognition feature.

Without question Mack's dual reduction rear axle with its multiple gear sets was an expensive design. The earlier worm gear rear end had accomplished the same gearing reduction, so what were the reasons for the expense of dual reduction? First, a worm rear drive lacks the efficiency and does not allow the speed range of bevel gears. Second, by angling the banjo obliquely to the rear casting, Mack's dual reduction rear axle gained an inch of ground clearance over the former worm design. The dual reduction rear axle gave 10-1/4in of ground clearance as opposed to 9-1/4in for the worm drive. Still, as would be expected from Mack, the main reason for designing the dual reduction rear axle was its extreme ruggedness and durability.

In a normal, single reduction hypoid rear axle, the drive pinion (a beveled gear attached to the end of the driveshaft) engages the differential ring gear. The ratio between the number of teeth on the drive pinion and ring gear determines the gearing ratio. For example, if there are nine teeth on the pinion and thirty-seven teeth on the ring gear, then the truck has a rear axle ratio of 4.1:1. Said another way, the driveshaft spins 4.1 times to each revolution of the rear axles. One of the reasons Mack designed the dual reduction rear axle is because a medium- or heavy-duty truck needs a large numerical differential ratio. To achieve the necessary reduction, not only does the ring gear need to be large, but also the entire torque of the engine must be able to be applied against one pair of gears that engage on a lateral mesh. Two problems arise from these demands. First, the large

The AB's most exceptional feature is a dual reduction rear axle introduced in 1920 as a replacement for worm gear rear drive.

ring gear requires a larger rear axle pumpkin, which lowers the truck's ground clearance. Second, applying all the engine torque against a ring and pinion gearset, which then drives the axle through small spider gears as is the case in traditional single reduction rear axles, increases the risk of stripping or damaging the gears—particularly given metallurgical capabilities of the early 1920s.

Mack's solution, the dual reduction rear axle, addressed both problems. As noted previously, ground clearance was raised by the obliquely angled rear axle banjo—something that would not have been possible in a single reduction hypoid rear axle. Also, the dual reduction design eliminated the spider gears, which single reduction axles use to transfer power from the ring gear to the axles, while also de-

In 1930 a six-cylinder version joined the four-cylinder AB model. Both engines were supplied with either the 146-1/2in or 164-1/2in wheelbase.

creasing the gearing ratio between the pinion and ring gears. To see the benefits clearly, let's look at how the dual reduction axle works.

Power arrives at the rear axle in the traditional manner through a pinion gear at the end of the driveshaft. As described previously, the bevels of this pinion gear mesh with the teeth of the ring gear. The ring gear, however, does not engage the axles. Rather, it turns a spur gear (attached to the ring gear casing), which meshes into a large bull gear located inside the banjo housing. The spur gear is small in relationship to the bull gear giving a steep (large numerical) second reduction. The teeth of both gears are straight cut for maximum strength. Finally, the axles lock directly into the bull gear. What happens

through dual reduction, then, is that power from the engine is transferred to the axles in a two-step process that reduces gear strain, eliminates the need for very large ring gear, and provides the final drive gearing needed for a truck burdened with heavy loads.

In addition to all the design pluses mentioned so far, Mack's dual reduction final drive offered one more benefit that helped extend the longevity of the truck. The one-piece, drop-forged axle housing made of alloy steel extended fully from hubcap to hubcap, and in so doing, this rugged housing carried the truck's weight. This design, where the housing and not the drive mechanism supported the weight of the truck and its load, was called a "full floating" axle.

On both chain-drive and gear-drive AB Macks, the rear brakes are the internal expanding type. Internal brakes have the advantage of being protected by the drums from dust and dirt, oil, and water. Rear brake drums on AB Macks through the 1920s measured an ample 18in in diameter while the brake linings had the 3-1/2in width facing. The brake drums are bolted to the spokes, thereby reinforcing the wheels. On later AB Series trucks, a vacuum booster aided braking action. A secondary braking device mounted on the driveshaft could be applied to keep the truck from rolling when parked. On trucks with the dual reduction axle, the driver applied this shaft brake by pulling back on a lever while the wheel brakes were applied by pressing on the brake pedal. According to Mack literature, on chain-drive trucks the brake mechanisms were reversed—the driver pulled back on the lever to engage the wheel brakes and pushed on the brake pedal to apply the shaft brake.

AB Macks used familiar semi-elliptical springs, which stretch almost flat in an unloaded state and show a slight reverse camber under full load. Several wheelbase lengths were offered. In 1930, a six-cylinder version joined the four-cylinder model. By this time the four-cylinder's power rating had been boosted to 58hp, while the six-cylinder carried a 78hp rating. Both engine versions were built on 146-1/2in and 164-1/2in wheelbases.

Standard equipment on these trucks included side and taillights, a canvas tool roll with 25 tools, as well as a jack and tool box. Beginning in 1921, electric starting and lights became available as special equipment. The starter motor and generator were Leece-Neville units. Buyers could choose among three cab styles: an open cab that gave no weather protection to the driver but afforded excellent visibility; a C cab, which added the weather-protecting benefits of a windshield and roof; or a fully enclosed cab complete with doors and roll-down windows. The C cab design proved popular because the open sides allowed easy entrance and exit and kept the driver well ventilated in warm weather operation. Roll-down side curtains could be installed to seal the cab from the elements in cold weather operation. Early enclosed cabs were largely of wooden construction; on later AB Macks, particularly those restyled to resemble the B Series, the enclosed cabs used all-metal construction.

AB chassis could be fitted with a wide variety of bodies such as low-sided express boxes, flat beds, and dump bodies, including the high-lift dump boxes used by coal delivery companies. The AB chassis also carried fuel tanks, fully enclosed furniture van bodies, and in a number of instances was fitted as a fire apparatus. In the early 1920s, to meet the need for flexible mass transit, motor bus companies were formed, and soon builders of medium-duty trucks

Beginning in 1921, the AB offered electric starting and lights as standard equipment. Note the location of the lights on the cowl of this truck. International Harvester

also mounted the lights on its 1920s Speed trucks in this
somewhat unusual location.

Most ABs wear the open C cab. The truck shown here is a 1930 model.

had a new market for truck chassis as platforms for bus bodies. However, these truck chassis used solid rubber tires that gave a harsh, jarring ride. In 1921 Mack developed the Mack Shock Insulated Bus, which used patented rubber shock insulators to help insulate bus passengers from the bumps and jounces transmitted to the chassis by solid rubber tires.

With the development of pneumatic truck tires, the bus's future became more promising. Mack developed a special low-slung AB Series chassis specifically for bus use. This chassis was fitted with two styles of bus bodies: a city bus used on urban routes and a sedan style used for intercity travel. The sedan model had low lines and looked like an elongated limousine. Its styling was designed to provide comfortable distance travel. As an alternative to chain or

dual reduction drive, Mack developed a special electric-drive AB bus chassis, which used the gasoline engine to drive an electrical generator that supplied current to electric motors at each driveshaft. An electric-drive bus would have been much easier to drive on stop-and-go city routes since the driver needed only to vary the current to the electric motors rather than be constantly shifting gears as would be the case with mechanical-drive chassis.

During the late '20s and early '30s, AB models were built with shortened chassis for use as tractors for semitrailers; but like the AC, the AB was not well suited to distance operation on improved highways. After all, the AB's design dated to the early part of the century when paved roads were nearly unknown. Accordingly its distinguishing features were

A 1928 Model AB dump truck with a fully enclosed cab. Although Mack built over 51,000 ABs during this Series 23-year production run, these trucks are not especially plentiful today.

its ruggedness and durability, not its speed—although AB semi-tractor models equipped with six-cylinder engines from the newly designed B Series trucks did serve quite well in this capacity.

With the introduction of the 1-1/2-ton BB model in 1928, one would have thought that Mack had slated the AB for retirement. Oddly, however, the AB continued in production —with revised sheet metal and other improvements from the new B line— while the BB survived only until 1932. In 1930, the AB had to surrender its title as the "Baby Mack" to

the new 1-ton BL model because no corresponding light-duty chassis had existed in the AB line since 1918. At the same time that the AB relinquished its light-duty claim, trucks from this series became available with the six-cylinder engine from the new BG model. The availability of this more powerful six-cylinder extended the life of AB Series' six more years with production of what had been the original Mack finally ceasing in 1936. With a manufacturing span of twenty-four years, the AB tied the AC in longevity but set a Mack truck sales record that still

The Mack 29-Passenger City Bus

The Model AB City Type

A special chassis, designed solely for bus work, with optional wheelbases of 196 and 225 inches. The former is mounted with a 25-passenger and the latter with a 29-passenger pay-enter bus body, built completely in the Mack factories. Interior view is shown at the left

The Parlor Car Type

For long-distance transit, the bus chassis, with 230½-inch wheelbase, is equipped with a luxurious, pay-center type body, whose beauty and completeness of appointments are only suggested by the inside and outside glimpses below and to the right

The Mack 25-Passenger Parlor Car Bus

With the development of pneumatic tires, Mack designed a special low-slung chassis for its AB Series trucks on which to mount bus bodies. The intercity bus, called the Parlor Car Type in this display, had a particularly handsome, almost streamlined, styling.

stands today. In addition to 51,613 AB Series trucks, Mack built 3,813 AB buses and six AB railcars, giving a total for all vehicles based on the AB design of 55,432. Clearly, Edward R. Hewitt and his staff of engineering designers had done their jobs well.

Today AB Series Macks are superseded by the distinctive AC "Bulldog" models as collector favorites; but the AC's popularity doesn't detract from the AB's appeal as an equally well-designed truck with many distinctive features. As is the case with vintage cars, early AB models with their brass radiators draw more attention than the later painted-radiator models; also the earlier truck with their lower radiators have a more "integrated" look than models of the 1923 through early 1930s period with radiators that stood slightly taller than the hood and had a grafted-on look. The sleekest members of the AB family are, of course, the intercity sedan-style buses.

Despite their high production numbers, ABs are not plentiful trucks. The few remaining are either in museums or turn out at major truck shows. If you're a vintage truck enthusiast, you'll find a great deal about the AB to admire. When you find one, look it over closely and reflect on its design that took less than a year to infuse into a running truck. If it's a chain-drive model, admire the "chain gang" mechanism. If it's fitted with the dual reduction rear axle, admire the complexity of the rugged power transfer unit. You may want to even take a few snapshots because it's unlikely that you'll see another AB Mack again soon.

The younger generation would probably mistake the high lift dump body on this AB Mack with a "trick" box on a modern mini-pickup. But in the early part of this century when most businesses and homes were heated by coal, the high-lift dump mechanism allowed coal to be chuted down into the customer's coal bin without having to manually shovel the coal off the truck.

Chapter 3

Mack AC "Bulldog"

The Mack AC is probably the most famous model Mack ever built and the source of the famous Mack Bulldog nickname and mascot. When I first became aware of the Mack AC, I pegged the truck I was looking at as a pre-1920s model. I dated the truck from its rugged, simple styling, open C cab, and chain drive. To my surprise—shock is probably a better word—the owner explained that his truck had been built in the late 1920s, a period I associated with closed cabs and a less primitive styling, marked by a prominent, brightmetal-plated radiator grille and shaft drive.

As I grew more familiar with the legendary AC, I learned that my initial hunch has been partly correct, at least to the extent that the Mack AC's design hailed from the mid-teens—1915, with production models appearing in 1916, to be exact. In fact, the AC was quite modern for that period. The unorthodox radiator-behind-engine location was actually quite fashionable in the mid-teens. The design had been introduced by Renault on both cars and trucks and used in the United States on trucks by International and Stewart as well as Mack. The prevailing legend explaining the radiator 's location behind the engine has it that in their rage over being put out of business by trucks, teamsters would "accidentally" back their wagons into the front of a competitor's truck, smashing the radiator, and putting the truck out of business. One look at the massive front cross-member on a Bulldog would quickly dissuade a horse and wagon handler from any such mischief on this truck, which would probably do more damage to the rear of the wagon than to the front of the truck.

Maybe such stories are more fiction than fact. Mack's sales literature found tangible benefits to the aft-mounted radiator. These benefits included better engine accessibility, reduced shock and vibration (which could cause the solder joints to flex and break, causing water leakage), and better weight distribution due to the radiator's position behind rather than in front of the front wheels. Then, too, there was the advantage of improved forward visibility for the driver whose view ahead of the truck wasn't obstructed by a massive radiator. As an added benefit, the radiator's location just ahead of the cowl provided heat for the driver in wintertime. (Coincidentally, nothing is said of the effect of the radiator's heat in summertime.) The sales literature also points out that the aft-mounted radiator allowed the steering gear to be placed ahead of the front axle, improving steering ease and allowing a lower angle of slope to the steering column. This list of benefits supports the view that Mack engineers hadn't selected its nontraditional location just to put the fragile radiator out of harm's way.

As anyone who has worked on big trucks will quickly recognize, placing the radiator behind the engine has a further plus—the engine and all its accessories are within easy reach when one lifts the rear-hinged hood. No one needs to climb up on the fenders or perch inside the engine compartment to perform routine upkeep or even more major overhauls to the powerplant of an AC Mack.

The second famous legend, how the Bulldog got its nickname, can also be traced to the unorthodox radiator location and sloping coal scuttle-shaped hood. In the spring of 1917, with World War I raging in Europe, the British government placed an order for 150 5-1/2-ton Mack AC chassis for use by the military. These trucks distinguished themselves so well, even in the most rigorous testing conditions, that the British army engineers gave them the endearing nickname "Bull Dog"; which to an Englishman represents the epitome of toughness and fight. But the Bulldog

What set Mack trucks apart from their competition was their unsurpassed engineering and quality parts that were built to Mack standards in Mack factories.

MANUFACTURED

—built, *not assembled*

The vital parts of the MACK chassis —axles, engine, transmission, frame, radiator, etc.—are built and finished at the MACK plants. Their refinements in design, materials and construction account for MACK superiority in power, strength, stamina, economical operation and reliable performance.

Per ton of rated capacity, MACK Trucks have the most powerful engines. The crankshafts are the largest and strongest used in any motor trucks. Chain drive delivers more power to rear wheels under all conditions than is possible with any other present form of drive.

Capacities 1½ to 7½ tons—tractors to 15 tons Special bodies and mechanical equipment.

The AC's most prominent and distinguishing feature is its Renault-style sloping hood that sits ahead of the radiator. Several other early trucks used this unorthodox behind-the-engine radiator location, including International and Stewart. Note that this 1920 vintage AC has solid rubber tires.

nickname becomes even more meaningful when one remembers that the wrinkle-snouted dog is to an Englishman what Uncle Sam is to an American—a national symbol. Of course the AC Mack's blunt, determined-looking frontal styling surely suggested the comparison to an Englishman's favorite dog, but the AC Mack certainly earned the endearing nickname by its reputation for performance, stamina, and longevity. What's important is that the nickname stuck and Macks have been known for the tenacious dog's fight and grit ever since.

As just mentioned, it wasn't just the AC's pug-nosed styling that earned the Bulldog nickname. The AC's engineering and design reflects nothing short of genius. First, great emphasis was placed on metallurgy, an emerging science, to give the AC Mack the

greatest possible strength with the lightest possible weight. Henry Ford also employed the science of metallurgy in designing the Model T, thanks to the genius of Childe Harold Wills. Using strong, lighter weight alloy steels, Ford's Model T, though as spindly looking as a newborn colt, took the punishment that destroyed more expensive, supposedly better-built cars. Today more Model Ts still exist than all other car makes of the time combined. The AC Mack showed the same kind of durability; and even though ACs are not nearly as common as Model Ts, it would be unusual to visit a gathering of antique trucks without seeing at least one "chain gang" AC Mack on display.

Like Ford and his Model T, Mack Chief Engineer Edward R. Hewitt, who oversaw the AC's development, designed the frame so that it could flex and twist without stressing and cracking the metal. The frame's flexibility was achieved by pressing the frame channels from chrome nickel steel that was later heat treated for toughness. Many cars and trucks of the day rode on rigid frames with designs that suffered two serious flaws. First, the rigid frame resulted in a harsher, more jarring ride. Second, a rigid frame placed great stress on suspension and other components as well as the frame itself whenever the vehicle moved over uneven ground. A flexible frame allowed a heavily burdened AC Mack to move smoothly over even the roughest footing.

Besides using strong alloy steel for critical chassis members, the AC Mack's designers also made use of aluminum wherever this lightweight metal had application. Uses of aluminum included the radiator tanks, transfer case, timing cover, and engine crankcase. By design, all these components were nonstressed, allowing the lighter, more brittle metal's use without sacrificing durability. In the crankcase, ribs were added for rigidity and each casting was carefully inspected for sand holes, which would have allowed oil leakage.

Along with special metals, Mack employed techniques to strengthen the key components such as the engine cylinders, pistons, crankcase, axles, and drive sprockets by heat treating. This process by which parts are placed in ovens and heated to high temperatures and then gradually allowed to cool is time consuming and expensive; however, it resulted in much stronger metal structures. Heating allowed the molecules in a preworked part to realign, relieving strains placed in the metal during earlier machining processes. The slow cooling preserved this realignment and prevented shrinkage, which would throw off critical tolerances. After heat treating, the engine cylinders, which were cased in pairs, were burnished to a smooth glazed finish to reduce friction and prevent oil consumption. Heat treating the AC Mack's engine cylinders resulted in much longer engine life by compacting the metal and preventing warpage that would otherwise occur from the cylinder castings' continuous heating and cooling during service. Compacting molecules in the metal castings led to greater durability, eliminating warpage of this major engine part, which also helped forestall out-of-round cylinders, misaligned bearings, or cracks—any of which would significantly shorten engine life. The AC Mack's legendary engine durability was due, in large part, to the heat treating process used to prepare the engine cylinder castings for long service.

The AC Mack engine used pistons made of gray cast iron, which were also heat treated like the cylinder castings. With these parts, heat treating enabled Mack to hold fine tolerances and significantly reduce wear. Another critical engine part, the crankshaft, re-

ceived a case-hardening treatment that left the journals surfaces so tough they could barely be scratched with a file and so smooth that, as long as the engine had proper lubrication, bearing life would be greatly extended. Case hardening also assured that the crankshaft would maintain its trueness, which also extended engine life.

Aside from the engine, other critical parts of a heavy-duty truck are the drive mechanism and axles. It should come as no surprise that Mack used special alloys and metal-strengthening processes with these parts, too. As already mentioned, all AC models used chain drive—a much less trouble-prone means of transferring power than shaft drive for several reasons. One of the major benefits of chain drive was elimination of the use of a casting for the rear axle. On the AC Mack the axle for the rear wheels inserts into a virtually unbreakable drop-forged billet of alloy steel. Moving forward through the driving mechanism, the torque handling capabilities of an AC Mack's roller chains far exceeds that of a shaft drive. To extend driveline life still further, the forward sprockets are case hardened, making them practically impervious to wear. According to sales literature for the AC Mack, field experience showed the front drive sprockets to be tough enough to outwear two sets of chains. Similar metallurgy also made the rear drive sprockets practically indestructible.

Although the front axle supported only the truck's forward weight, it received thoughtful design care. On heavy-duty trucks used in rough terrains

On very early ACs, the side hood panels are screened. Most AC hoods use louvers on the side panels for ventilation. This all-original truck is from the AC's first year of production, 1916.

like construction sites or the floor of a quarry, front axle damage from hitting rocks or surface outcroppings is likely. Along with the chance of actually breaking an axle, there is the greater risk of bending the axle and throwing the front wheels out of track, which makes the truck much harder to steer and causes handling problems that make the truck unsafe to drive. The AC's designers took two steps that make front axle damage on these trucks extremely rare. First, the front axle is made of extremely strong drop-forged alloy steel. Second, the axle's shape is a continuous curve, which means there are no bends to serve as weak points. Besides making the axle tough enough to withstand damage, the AC's designers also used the front axle as a shield for the tie-rod mounted behind the axle. A bent tie-rod distorts steering even more than a bent axle.

Achieving the desired function through the simplest possible design is said to be the real mark of engineering genius. Using this standard, the Mack AC evidences numerous examples of design excellence. For example, the radiator location (a design feature already mentioned) not only gave the truck its distinctive look, but also allowed unsurpassed accessibility to the engine and its accessories. Lifting the hood put the engine, water pump, and magneto in full view and within easy reach. In fact, easy access to critical components is a hallmark of the AC Mack design. Unbolting the front frame cross-member exposed the engine's timing cover, which could then be removed to service the governor or replace the timing gear in the unlikely event that the drop-forged and case-hardened timing gear ever needed to be replaced. Removable covers on the left side of the

This 1928 AC has the more common style of louvered hood along with pneumatic tires.

A combination of the aft-mounted radiator and front-opening hood gave easy access to the engine, as on this 1919 AC. Another advantage of the radiator's location di- *rectly in front of the cab was that in wintertime the driver could remove a cover on the blower cage and enjoy a steady blast of warm air.*

crankcase allowed visual inspection of the connecting rod and main bearings. The oil pump could be reached from outside the crankcase, and no teardown was required to replace the clutch.

Needless to say, easy access to critical mechanical parts means shorter equipment downtimes when repairs are needed. But the AC's designers also helped forestall repairs, not only by using premium materials, but also by putting lubrication points within easy access. Before the days of neoprene bushings and "lifetime" lubricants, frequent greasing and oiling of moving parts was critical to their survival. A truck whose lubrication points were difficult to reach got little replenishment of vital lubricants. But if lubrication was easy, an operator was far more likely to pay attention to this critical detail.

The AC's design was so innovative, it was covered by eighteen basic patents. Cunning design details are seen in numerous areas. Both the engine's front and rear main bearing caps tie into rugged steel beams that support the engine. Using the engine's support structure to secure the crankshaft had two benefits. First, it freed the aluminum crankcase from any support function, allowing this light metal casting to serve only as an oil reservoir. Second, bolting the front and rear crankshaft bearing caps to the engine's rugged support structures kept the crankshaft in perfect alignment regardless of stress on chassis parts, thereby extending bearing and engine life.

Another clever design feature can be seen on the right side of the engine where a double-cored intake manifold circulates engine coolant around the vaporized fuel/air mixture to prevent gasoline from condensing on cold intake manifold surfaces causing hard starting and power loss. For cold weather starting, air drawn into the starter is preheated by a simple, yet ingenious "exhaust stove" consisting of a cast aluminum jacket bolted around the exhaust pipe just below the pipe's connection to the exhaust manifold. A valve, operated from a control knob on the

The AC got its famous "Bulldog" nickname from its imposing, stubby-nosed appearance, as well as its stamina and toughness.

dashboard, allows the truck's operator to close off the "exhaust stove" so that cooler air will be drawn into the carburetor once the engine warms up. Although preheated air is useful for starting because it allows better fuel vaporization, cooler air, which is more dense, delivers greater combustion volume and thereby more power, which is desirable once the engine is warmed up.

Although the smoothly cast exhaust manifold with its cooling fins looks borrowed from an expensive racing car, the AC's engineers never let "beauty" be only skin deep. Just as the intake manifold casting contained dual passages for fuel and water, the exhaust manifold also employed dual passages, but for a different reason. Here, one passage scavenged exhaust for cylinders 1 and 4 while the other passage carried away spent fuel gases from cylinders 2 and 3. Why design a manifold within a manifold you may

be asking. The reason has to do with what happens at the end of an engine's power cycle. Even in engines with relatively slow rpm like those found in the AC, before a cylinder where combustion has just occurred has a chance to completely purge its exhaust gases, another cylinder has fired and is also dumping its exhaust. When two cylinders are emptying into the exhaust manifold simultaneously, back pressure forms that prevents some of the spent, but still very hot gases from escaping the cylinder. These gases, which contain very little oxygen and no fuel, displace some of the cylinder area that could otherwise be filled with a fresh fuel/air mixture and reduce the incoming gases' cooling effect on the cylinder. The result is not only power loss but also hotter operation of critical engine parts. The dual passage design of the AC's exhaust manifold eliminated this back pressure because adjacent cylinders dumped into openings that didn't merge until they neared the manifold's outlet. Further, by "tuning" the length of the exhaust passages to the duration of the exhaust strokes, the AC's designers set up a partial vacuum at the exhaust port that actually helped suck spent gases out of the cylinder. The concept is simple and its execution elegant.

As with so many facets of the AC's design, the cooling system is an engineering marvel. The radiator, which mounts in a secure position behind the engine as has already been described, consists of 154 tubes in two sections—one on the left and the other on the right side of the truck—each comprised of seventy-seven tubes set in eleven rows, seven tubes deep. Each cooling tube measures 25-5/8in in length and 3/8in in diameter. At the top and bottom, these tubes are soldered to header plates to which the top and bottom tanks are bolted, with gaskets sandwiched in between. The tanks are made of cast aluminum for maximum ruggedness and minimum weight. In the top tank, access doors make it possible to rod out the tubes—run a cleaning rod down through the radiator tubes to clean out mineral scaling or other deposits—as well as clean buildup from around the outsides of the tubes that may have restricted cooling without requiring that the radiator be removed from the truck. The bottom tanks connect by a copper tube. Beneath the radiator, a 21in di-

Right
A large measure of Mack's legendary reliability results from building its own engines. The attention to detail lavished on the AC engine included heat-treating the engine block and case-hardening the crankshaft for long service. One of the AC's clever design features can be seen on the right side of the engine where a double-cored intake manifold preheats the fuel charge before it arrives at the cylinders.

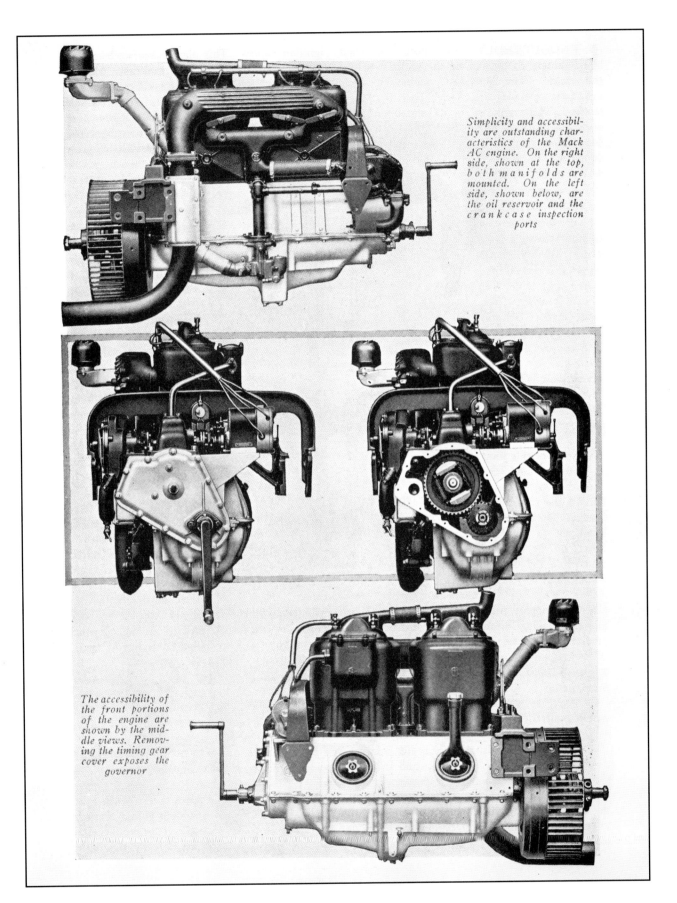

Simplicity and accessibility are outstanding characteristics of the Mack AC engine. On the right side, shown at the top, both manifolds are mounted. On the left side, shown below, are the oil reservoir and the crankcase inspection ports

The accessibility of the front portions of the engine are shown by the middle views. Removing the timing gear cover exposes the governor

The general arrangement of the radiator is shown in these views as well as the mounting of the blower on the flywheel, one of the cooling sections, the blower and air duct separately, and some of the accessibility features

ameter squirrel cage blower (early ACs used a belt-driven fan) mounted directly to the clutch shaft draws air in from the rear and blows it up through the space between the two sets of tubes and out through the sides of the radiator. The massive air flow generated by the squirrel cage blower is more than adequate to keep an AC Mack from overheating even under the hardest working conditions and in the most torrid climates.

The Bulldog Mack's aft-mounted radiator had another benefit appreciated by the truck's operators. Hot air from the radiator could be ducted into the cab to warm the driver when the mercury had dropped. Since most ACs were fitted with open C cabs that had a draftiness about them even when canvas side curtains had been snapped in place, receiving some of the radiator's warmth made for much more comfortable working conditions during cold weather operation.

The radiator design also accommodated cold weather operation by providing shutters at the outside of both sets of cooling tubes. By working a lever from inside the cab, the driver could open or close the shutters to maintain coolant temperature. Closing the shutters also protected the radiator from cold air drafts when the truck was shut off.

Coolant circulated from the radiator to the engine by means of a water pump that also reflected thoughtful design. To give this component long life, stainless steel was specified for the water pump shaft. Besides being noncorrosive, stainless steel is an extremely hard metal so shaft wear at the bushing areas, which is prevalent on water pumps using plain steel shafts, is virtually eliminated. To further extend the life of this vital component, Mack's engineers designed the pump rotor, made of noncorrosive navy bronze, in such a way that it draws water from both sides so as to eliminate any side thrust that would speed bearing and bushing wear. Details of this sort, which are so often overlooked, mark the difference between a Bulldog and just a truck.

From the water pump, the coolant passes through the intake manifold to prevent fuel condensation as previously mentioned. Then it enters the cylinder blocks where circulation passages direct the coolant to the exhaust valves. The purpose of this flow pattern is to bring the coolant at its coldest temperature to the hottest part of the engine. Normal practice brings water into the head and, then from there, down into the cylinders. The AC Mack uses a reverse approach,

Note the side curtains fitted to this AC's C cab to protect the driver and passenger from the elements.

drawing the warmed water out of the head. But here again, we see the designer's genius in directing the coolant first to where its cooling potential is needed most. The result is a much more even operating temperature for the engine, which helps prevent heat buildup from distorting the casting and thereby reduces wear and prolongs engine life.

The design innovations incorporated into the AC Mack don't stop with the engine and cooling system. A small ring of friction material attached to the clutch sleeve presses against the forward universal joint flange when the clutch is disengaged and quickly stops the clutch from spinning. Why not let the clutch continue to "free wheel" when released as it does in other vehicles you may ask. The reasons suggest themselves. Braking the spinning clutch no doubt reduces clutch sleeve wear at the same time it ensures smooth shifting without clashing unevenly spinning gears.

As part of its chain-drive design, the AC combines the transmission with the differential and houses both units in an integrated housing made of high-strength aluminum alloy. Early ACs were fitted with three-speed transmission, but a four-speed gearbox that replaced the three-speed in 1922 gave the advantage of an ultra-low first gear for crawling out of a coal pit or inching along a logging track.

All AC Macks used chain drive—a feature that is as much a part of the Bulldog Mack's legend as is the sloping hood. Chain drive might have seemed necessary for drive-line strength when the AC was

Left

As with so many facets of the AC's design, the cooling system is an engineering marvel. The radiator, which is constructed in two parts, actually straddles the rear of the engine.

With the side curtains rolled up, the C cab gave lots of ventilation and visibility.

first introduced in 1915, but this model continued into production through 1930 when shaft drive had been adopted almost universally. So why did Mack persist, and in fact favor, chain drive? Actually, chain drive offered the AC several advantages. First, even given the best metallurgy of the day, chain drive provided far greater strength and less risk of driveline failure than shaft drive for larger capacity trucks. Second, drive reduction could be raised or lowered easily by changing the front sprockets. Third, a solid beam rear axle proved nearly indestructible in quarries where loose stones and rock outcroppings could crack a rear axle casting. Fourth, mounting the differential high on the

frame with the transmission eliminated the low-hanging banjo rear axle necessitated by shaft drive, which had proved vulnerable not just in quarries, but on any uneven road surface.

Although the AC used external contracting brakes at the rear wheels with stopping effectiveness that could deteriorate in rain and mud, the brakes could easily be kept in proper tension by the operator or a mechanic turning large wing nuts on the ends of the brake rods. One advantage of the external contracting brakes is that the friction material is more easily replaced than on internal contracting brakes where the chains and brake drums must first be removed.

Unlike the arched springs found on some heavy-duty trucks, the rear springs used on the AC are nearly flat. The lack of an arch or curve suggests that the springs deflect very little under fully loaded conditions. This is true, but it does not mean that the springs are inflexible nor that they give a stiff ride. The long, wide spring leaves are made of a strong, yet flexible electric furnace chrome silica-magnesium steel. Because the AC's frame is also made of flexible steel, a high spring arch is not needed to allow for wheel deflection on uneven road surfaces. The flat springs are actually more flexible and therefore do a better job of cushioning the load and driver than arched springs. They also have the advantage of allowing minimum side sway, which is important in the safe operation of a loaded truck. Under fully loaded conditions, the rear springs on an AC Mack will show some slight deflection.

Thanks to its many superb design features, the AC Mack is one of the easiest-to-operate large trucks of the period. For the most part the controls are similar to those found on other trucks built in the 1920s.

For trucks operated in severe climates, Mack offered a fully enclosed cab, as on this 1920. Note that in addition to the all-weather cab, this truck is also fitted with electric lights.

Both spark and throttle control levers are mounted on the steering wheel with the levers pressing against a ratchet quadrant. Many drivers of the period preferred to control engine speed by the throttle lever rather than by the foot accelerator—using the accelerator pedal for maneuvering in traffic or on the job site and the throttle lever for open-road travel. The spark lever retards or advances the engine's ignition firing position. The spark is retarded during engine starting and advanced once the engine is running to enable the engine to deliver full power. Although the clutch and brake pedals are in their usual positions, the accelerator is located in an unusual position between the pedals for the clutch and brake. A driver wouldn't accidentally put his foot on the accelerator thinking it was the clutch because of the much larger pedal size for both the clutch and brake. But rather than press against the accelerator with the right foot, which is customary on most cars and trucks, the AC driver could operate the accelerator with the left foot. A large aluminum footrest on the floorboard below the accelerator pedal gave a relax-

ing shoe anchor for drivers who preferred to control their truck's engine speed on highway travel with the accelerator. The larger clutch and brake pedals both had tangs on their outer edges to prevent a driver's shoe or boot from slipping off the pedal during shifting or braking. Gear shifting was handled by a long nickel-plated lever mounted in the usual position in the center of the floor. The parking brake lever stood immediately to the right of the gearshift.

The science that we call ergonomics, which measures a design's effectiveness by its ease of use, had not been developed when the AC took shape on the engineers' drawing boards; yet, ergonomically sound features can be found in many facets of the AC's design. From the driver's point of view, one of the features that most clearly shows the designer's attempt to limit driver fatigue and discomfort is seen in the construction of the steering wheel.

Since it is impossible to isolate the driver of a solid-tired vehicle from vibrations transmitted though the steering mechanism, Mack set about to cushion the steering wheel to prevent operators' hands from

The C cab could also be supplied without a windshield. Trucks with this style cab were often fitted with isinglass curtains that could be rolled down to protect the driver in bad weather. However, since the isinglass areas couldn't be kept clear with windshield wipers, this arrangement made for poor visibility in rainy or snowy weather.

Mack offered the AC in 3-1/2, 5, and 7-1/2 ton load ratings with wheelbases ranging from 156in to 240in. The AC shown here is a 7-1/2 ton 1926 model.

going numb due to constant shaking as they gripped the steering wheel. Rather than the solid wood core used for most steering wheels of the day, the AC's wheel is built around a core of flexible steel tubing. Around this core, cotton fabric and rubber are wound in plies to build up a cushiony covering. To protect this cushion from the elements, a final layer of rubber is applied. The result is a steering wheel that is springy to the touch but still affords the driver a surface that doesn't become slippery, even when soaked with water or begrimed with grease or oil. The rubber covering even provides a good gripping surface in the wintertime when operators protect their hands from the cold with woolen gloves. No doubt Mack's thoughtfulness in designing a steering

wheel that didn't cause the driver's hands to slip and cushioned out annoying and physically troublesome vibrations helped build Mack loyalty.

Instrumentation on the AC is exceedingly sparse, consisting only of an oil gauge on the dashboard and a motometer mounted on top of the radiator filler cap located in clear view almost directly ahead of the oil gauge. Motometers, which consist of little more than a thermometer whose base inserts into the radiator and shows temperature through markings ascribed inside a glass face, were the standard temperature gauge for both cars and trucks of the period. To check fuel level the driver would have to lift the seat cushion and measure the amount of gasoline in the tank with a calibrated stick. Besides

In the early 1920s Mack built several rail cars using the AC engine for motive power. This is one of the most unusual AC Mack's you'll ever see.

containing the fuel tank, the boxed-in compartment on which the seat cushion perched also allowed space to store extra oil and lubricants as well as critical spare parts.

So that the driver could determine when his truck needed routine maintenance such as chassis lubrication or an oil change, the left front wheel hub carried an odometer. To help the operator remember all the lubrication points, two complete diagrams—one for the chassis and another for the engine—etched on heavy brass plates so as to be nearly indestructible, were mounted inside the cab. Although the AC had an odometer, it did not have a speedometer for the simple and logical reason that

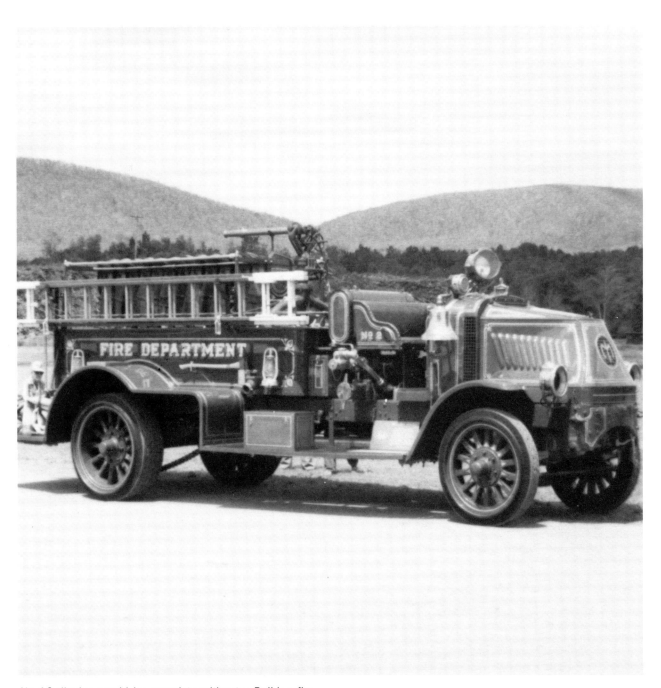

No AC display would be complete without a Bulldog fire apparatus. Note the rear fender extension to clear the chain drive.

Bulldog fire apparatus were popular with fire departments by virtue of their stamina and durability, not to mention their handsome appearance.

these trucks were not about to exceed any legal speed limit and the driver could better gauge appropriate speed by safety.

The AC came standard with an open cab consisting of a low enclosure that stopped at seat height. For a small extra charge, an AC could be optioned with a covered cab. It's important to note that a covered cab is not the same thing as an enclosed cab. Today we call the covered cab a C cab, referring to its open front and sides and the roof making a rough "C" shape as it projects out over the driver. Even though the covered C cab looks cold and drafty, particularly for drivers operating a covered cab AC in a northern climate, this style—which is most popular on restored trucks today—has certain advantages over the enclosed cab and is light years ahead of the

open cab in comfort. Actually, the C cab is not as open and drafty as it looks. Roll-down side and back window curtains were provided to keep out the weather. A canvas windshield curtain, fitted with isinglass windows, could be installed to protect the driver in front. With the covered cab "all buttoned up" the driver could work in relative comfort because even though the canvas curtains didn't have much insulating value, warm air ducted into the cab

Right
So durable was the AC that Mack could show this model, last built in 1938, in a 1949 ad inviting Mack owners to upgrade to a new truck.

from the radiator kept the enclosure warm in all but the most rigorous weather. Another advantage, with the side and back curtains rolled up and the front windshield curtain removed, the driver had the nearly panoramic visibility of an open cab. Mack intended the fully enclosed cab, which was of all-steel construction, for trucks operated in severe climates. Lacking windshield wipers, the enclosed cab had rather poor visibility in heavy rain and snow.

As electric starters and lights became available, Mack made this equipment optional on its AC trucks as accessories. When electric lights were fitted they were mounted between the front fender crowns and hood so as to be protected by the massive front cross-member. Other accessories and auxiliary equipment included a pintle hook, draw bar, power tire pump, and power takeoff.

Mack offered the AC in three load ratings: 3-1/2, 5, and 7-1/2 tons. Standard wheel bases ranged from 156in to 240in, with special lengths available to suit the customer. The four-cylinder AC engine displaced 471ci from a 5in bore and a 6in stroke. To say that an AC Mack had pistons the size of coffee cans makes a fairly accurate comparison. At governed speed, the Bulldog four-banger put out 50hp. At maximum speed the engine's power output increased to 74hp. Ignition was by magneto, and the wheels were cast steel. Virtually every imaginable body type could be adapted, from dumps to flatbed, van or bus to trailer-tractor, fire engine to water tanker. Wherever work needed to be done, an AC stood ready to do it.

Since Mack didn't identify the production year of its AC Series trucks by any sort of annual markings and made refinements and improvements whenever development and testing proved their merit, the only way to tell where an AC Mack fits into the model's 22-year production span—ACs were built from 1916 to 1938—is by production number sequence. In total, 40,299 ACs were built, making this model Mack's third largest seller behind the B61 with a production run of 47,459 trucks and the AB, which hit a production high of 51,613.

Improvements made to the AC included modifications to the radiator and a squirrel cage blower—attached to the flywheel in place of the former belt-driven fan and made in 1922 to aid cooling—and substitution of a four-speed transmission for the original three-speed gearbox later that year. In 1930, a more powerful six-cylinder engine became available. In 1932, the AC chassis received modifications required to accommodate pneumatic tires. From 1936 on, ACs were built only by special order—Mack had many customers loyal to the AC due to its incredible reputation for being able to take it under the most severe conditions. These so-called Custom Line trucks could be ordered with either a four-cylinder or six-cylinder gasoline engine or diesel-powered engine by Buda or Cummins. Most ACs built in the 1930s were equipped with fixed windshields, even when fitted with the C cab.

Mack's reason for designing the AC had been to supplement the AB with a heavier-duty truck line. The first AC prototype was driven as early as August 1915; however, production did not begin until early 1916. As mentioned earlier, even before the US entered World War I, Bulldog Macks were purchased for war use by the British. With America's entry into the war, more ACs were transported across the Atlantic. Mack's eventual production of ACs for military use exceeded 4,000 units.

The end of the war to end all wars put America in an expansive mood. In 1919, to demonstrate the use of trucks for military transport, the War Department conducted what it called the First Transcontinental Army Convoy. On July 7th of that year, a convoy of seventy-two vehicles, comprised mainly of trucks from different manufacturers, set out from Washington, D.C., headed for the West Coast. After two months of travel and enduring the hardships of several thousand miles over roadless terrain, the convoy arrived in San Francisco on September 6. Needless to say, several AC Macks had made the cross-country trek, some of which had been used by the Army Corps of Engineers to carry heavy timbers and other materials to shore up bridges along the way. This Transcontinental Army Convoy and other privately sponsored events focused the nation's attention on the need for roads. The 1920s became a boom era for road construction; many ACs saw service in road building and other public works.

As the expression has it, the AC became a legend in its own time. Today this model Mack is unquestionably the most sought after heavy-duty collector truck.

Chapter 4

AK and AP: Bulldog Cousins

As improved roads began to crisscross the countryside, connecting smaller towns as well as cities, Mack saw the need for a truck that combined the gear-driven rear axle of the AB with the hauling power of the AC. Less an AC/AB hybrid than an AC adapted to highway travel, the AK appeared in the fall of 1927. At first glance, an AK could easily be mistaken for a Bulldog (the name commonly given to the AC); and it's possible that modern-day Mack fanciers could make this recognition error, too. Mistaking an AK for an AC occurs because both share the Bulldog's Renault style hood with the radiator mounted at the engine's rear, as well as the C-style cab.

The easiest way to tell an AK from an AC is to look at the drive mechanism. Nearly all AKs have a shaft drive and dual reduction differential similar in design, though heavier-duty, to that used on the AB. (Recall that ACs were nearly universally chain driven.) Another telltale difference is the gas tank, which sat under the driver's seat in both models. On the AK, however, the tank had an external filler spout and tank gauge so that the seat cushion did not have to be lifted to fill the tank as was the case with the AC. And of course other less noticeable differences distinguished the two models. Early AKs wore solid rubber tires, but by 1929 nearly all were shod with pneumatics. To counter the higher speeds allowed by pneumatic tires, the AK employed four-wheel brakes. Another difference for those with an eye for detail was the AK's cast steel wheels that had the same number of spokes (six) front and rear. In contrast, ACs of similar vintage rode on steel wheels, with front and rear wheels having five and seven spokes respectively.

The early AKs also used a different engine—which had four cylinders like the AC—with all cylinders cast in a single block unlike the two separate castings for pairs of cylinders found on the earlier AC engines. The AK engine had a slightly smaller bore of 4-5/8in; the AC had a 5in bore. The AK used the same 6in stroke but had a power rating of 70hp, making it less powerful than the AC, which was showing a 74 hp rating by the mid-1920s. This early AK engine also featured an aluminum cylinder head.

Apparently this AK engine did not work. In 1928 Mack introduced an improved monoblock engine in the AC—which might have been based on the AK block, bored slightly larger—and in 1929, the AK adopted this engine. A distinguishing feature of this AC/AK engine is the rather thick aluminum alloy cylinder heads, which led to the nickname "high hat."

From the start, AK trucks were fitted with a four-speed transmission. Initially, the AK models carried load ratings of 3-1/2 to 5 tons, but in 1931 the capacity of this medium-duty highway series was raised from 5 to 8 tons. Mack marketed the AK as a faster truck in the moderate capacity range. To offset the increased speed, Mack added vacuum-boosted mechanical brakes.

As opposed to the rugged service settings in which the AC thrived, the AK found most of its use in urban areas working on a wide variety of tasks from street maintenance and snow removal to moving furniture and hauling produce. Besides shaft drive, several other features adapted the AK particularly well to inner city truck use. A shorter turning radius made the AK maneuverable in the tight confines of crowded alleys and cramped loading docks. Use of rubber as a shock absorber in the cab supports and spring brackets, combined with pneumatic tires, made the AK not only a more comfortable truck to drive but also helped cushion more fragile loads—such as furniture—against road shock. Rather than the open C cab so commonly found on AC Bulldog Macks, AKs were furnished with a covered cab fitted with a one- or two-piece, slightly slanted windshield. The AK's cab was also slightly larger than the corresponding covered cab offered on AC models.

When Mack began to upgrade its AC trucks with six-cylinder engines, a six-cylinder AK model also became available. This truck saw some use in the construction field as a shaft-drive alternative to the AC, but in off-road use chain drive proved more durable so the AK-6, as the six-cylinder model was called, saw limited sales. Its introduction in 1931 near the bottom of the Depression also curtailed this model's success. Altogether, Mack built 2,819 AK trucks, both four- and six-cylinder powered. The low production accounts largely for the lack of familiarity casual Mack enthusiasts have for this truck series. It also explains why, on the rare occasion that an AK model turns up at a truck show, most observers think they are seeing a shaft-drive AC.

Mack engineers began working on a six-cylinder engine in the early 1920s. Two needs motivated the development of a larger, more powerful engine. The expansion of paved highways that led to the shaft-drive AK also caused Mack to recognize the power and flexibility advantages offered by six-cylinder engines. Mack also looked in the direction of six cylinders for engines with sufficient stamina to power its bus, fire truck, and rail car operations.

By 1923, chief engineer A. F. Masury and his staff had developed Mack's first six-cylinder engine—a monstrous thing called the AH, with a bore and stroke of 5-1/3x7in and a power rating of 120hp. Although this engine proved cost prohibitive for use in trucks, Mack was also building rail cars and fire engines—applications where engine size and expense were less important than gross power. Still, the AH never saw production. In 1924, the engineering staff unveiled another six-cylinder called the AJ, this time with a smaller 4-1/4x6in bore and stroke rated at 100hp. This engine was installed in the Greatcoach, an experimental six-wheel bus. This engine, too, proved unsatisfactory for use in trucks, principally because its long stroke made it a low-speed motor. Development toward a workable six-cylinder engine continued and in 1926 a smaller 4-1/4x5in bore and stroke six-cylinder, called the AL, entered production. This engine, with its 97hp rating, found use in buses as well as fire engines based on the AC chassis. An AL Bulldog fire truck can be distinguished from its AC look-alike by additional louvers (thirteen rather than the usual ten) on the sides of the hood.

Mack's efforts in designing a practical six-cylinder engine had been motivated by the rapid expan-

The easiest way to tell an AK Mack from an AC is to look at the drive mechanism. AC's used chain drive universally while nearly all AKs have a shaft drive and dual reduction differential which is similar to, though heavier duty, than that used on the AB. Mack Museum

TRANSIT CONCRETE MIXED

LOIZEAUX
Builders Supply Co.
Elizabeth New Jersey

LOIZEAUX PHONE EMERSON 1776

Another tell-tale difference between the AK and AC is the gas tank filler location. On both models the gas tank lay under the seat, but the AK had an external filler spout and tank gauge so that the seat cushion did not have to be removed to fill the fuel tank. Mack Museum

The AK can also be recognized by an enclosed cab. Most AKs saw service in urban areas where they were used for a wide variety of functions from street maintenance and snow removal to moving furniture and hauling produce.

sion of paved highways, advances in pneumatic tires for trucks, plus changes in state laws that raised legal gross vehicle weight—all of which created a market for larger trucks with increased highway speeds. To pull heavier loads at higher speeds, six-cylinder engines were needed. Toward this end, in 1926 Mack introduced a new six-cylinder called the AP, which carried a much higher power rating of 150hp (nearly twice the power of a four-cylinder AC) and had an evenly matched bore and stroke of 6x6in. The AP saw its first application in a new series of fire apparatus, but in 1929 Mack introduced a new Bulldog-styled truck line using this monster engine.

The first production AP model carried loads of 7-1/2 tons at speeds up to 30mph. Unlike the AK, the heavier-duty AP also featured chain drive using the same drive components as the heaviest-rated AC model. Due to the near impossibility of hand cranking the huge engine, electric starting was provided as standard equipment. Likewise, in keeping with the load rating, vacuum-boosted mechanical brakes were also provided.

With the introduction of six-wheeled models and load ratings up to 10 tons, the AP became Mack's super-duty-model, quickly establishing a reputation for legendary Mack toughness under the most rugged settings. Although the AP wore the Bulldog's most familiar features, namely the aft-mounted radiator and chain drive, even a novice Mack admirer will often recognize an AP as something different than the more familiar AC. Probably the most readily noticed difference is the longer hood (needed for the six-cylinder engine). For those who like details, the AP hood was stamped with thirteen louvers on a side whereas the four-cylinder AC hood has ten louvers. It is also customary to differentiate an AP by its thicker radiator containing nearly twice as many rows of cooling tubes as the AC radiator. These differences are complicated, however, by Mack's introduction of a six-cylinder AC model in 1931—which

Six-cylinder AK models were fitted with a larger capacity radiator, which is easily spotted by the radiator's larger thickness caused by an increased number of cooling tubes.

used the BK six-cylinder engine until 1932, when the more powerful BK six was adopted by both the AC and AP—and Mack's decision to offer a four-cylinder version of the AP. As would be expected, the AC-6 used the AP-6's longer hood while the AP-4 used the short hood from the AC. The thicker radiator cannot always be used as a sure recognition feature as many AP models carry the thinner, AC-style radiator. Although not a sure difference, AKs were built with a greater mix of shaft-drive models than is the case with the AC.

In keeping with Mack's tradition of building its trucks to stand up to the work they are purchased to do, the AP design exuded ruggedness throughout. Vital mechanical parts were case hardened for durability. Camshafts were ground from unusually large steel billets. Crankshafts used in the powerful 150hp AP engines had both massive size and used counterbalancing to hold up under severe stress. Extreme ruggedness was also the watchword for the construction of the four-speed transmission, which contained gears of exceptional width and featured Mack's exclusive interrupted splineshaft design to accurately center and guide the gears to ensure a smooth mesh and maximum power transfer. AP models using chain drive also benefited from the extreme ruggedness of this final drive mechanism. Brakes, while still mechanical, were also of greater size and assisted by a vacuum booster. As would be expected, the frame on these heavy-duty trucks was a massive heat-treated steel structure. The springs also had a massiveness matching the truck's load capability.

To increase the AP's load capability, Mack developed six-wheel models. The first six-wheelers were fitted with a nonpowered bogie rear axle, but by 1931 Mack developed its Power Divider differential that gave driving power to both rear axles. Like the dual reduction rear axle, the Power Divider was a Mack exclusive. Located between the front and rear jackshafts, the Power Divider allowed one set of drive wheels to turn faster or slower than the other. (It's important that differences in drive wheel speed be allowed on trucks where tire diameters may vary and where uneven road surfaces may make the distance traveled by one set of drive wheels different than the other.) Besides this distance-compensating feature, the Power Divider provided another significant benefit to the operation of a primarily off-road truck. With an ordinary differential, power is supplied to the wheels having the least traction. That's why it is possible to get "stuck" when one set of wheels is on solid footing. With the Power Divider, a greater percentage of engine torque goes to the wheels having the most traction. The result is a truck that not only has the benefit of driving power from all rear wheels, but also provides superior traction over loose or soft terrain.

Mack's extensive use of rubber as shock absorbers for cab supports and spring brackets, combined with pneumatic tires, made the AK a relatively comfortable truck to drive. The "blocks" in the forefront of this photo are Mack rubber spring supports being sold at a swap meet held in conjunction with the Antique Truck Club of America's annual Macungie, Pennsylvania, truck show.

As would be expected of a Mack design, the Power Divider's design and construction was rugged throughout. The unit receives power from the main driveshaft. An extremely rugged six-lugged gear (called a "driving dog") at the splined end of the Power Divider's front pinion shaft meshes with teeth cut into the inside diameter of a sun-type gear called a "gyrating member." This gear then drives a forward-facing gear set to power the front pinion and jackshaft ring gear as well as a rearward-facing drive gear that transmits power to the rear jackshaft pinion and ring gears. A unique feature of the Power Divider's design is the "gyrating member," which is eccentric to the main shaft and finds its position relative to the gears it drives. This means that when differences in axle speeds occur due to uneven road surface or tire diameters, the gyrating member is free to rotate around the front and rear drive gears. Since the front gearset has twenty teeth and the rear gearset has nineteen teeth, one set will turn faster or slower than the other as required by operating conditions.

The operation by which the gyrating member transfers power to the two jackshafts also enables the Power Divider to limit wheel spin. When one set of wheels loses traction, power is prevented from flowing in that direction by drag that sets up when the gyrating member tries to roll around the driving gearsets too fast. The result is that the Power Divider does not allow either axle to spin freely, but transfers power in a somewhat even fashion to both axles at all times. The result is an efficient distribution of torque to all four driving wheels under all road conditions.

Mack called the Power Divider a third differential—which it is—but its function is to divide power front and rear rather than left and right. Besides the wonder of the Power Divider's own design, the design and construction of the two chain-driven wheel sets on a six-wheeler Super-Duty Mack is an exercise in mechanical artistry. The Power Divider mounts at the rear of the front jackshaft differential, which drives the chains to the front pair of drive wheels. Immediately behind this wheelset's axle is the differential for the rear jackshaft, which drives another set of chains to the rear wheels. For those who enjoy the duet of singing chains on an AC or AP Mack, the chorus of four whirring chains is music indeed.

Super-duty six-wheelers equipped with the Power Divider differential and four-rear wheel chain drive were offered in both AC four-cylinder and AP six-cylinder models. Few of these trucks were purchased for highway haulage. Most of the sales went to the construction industry where AP and AC super-duty models with load ratings up to 10 tons ex-

cavated the foundation for Rockefeller Center in New York City and helped construct the piers to the George Washington Bridge. Probably the most famous construction project built with the help of AP and AC super-duty trucks is the Hoover Dam. Here a fleet of more than twenty big Macks, including a dozen four-wheeler APs specially built for the project with 14yd rock bodies, helped move mountains of rock on a schedule that called for the equipment to work in continuous operation twenty-four hours a day in temperatures that ranged from zero in the winter to over 110 degrees in summer. The super-duty Mack fleet proved able to meet the challenge and served as Mack's lead into the off-highway truck market.

Mack AP Mixer 1929-1938

The AP represented Mack's Super Duty model, quickly establishing a reputation for legendary Mack toughness under the most demanding conditions. To increase load capacity, Mack developed six-wheeler models that were built in both its AP and AC Series.

Mack's exclusive, patented Power Divider, seen here in an exploded view, directs a greater percentage of engine torque to the wheels having the most traction. The Power Divider's ability to keep a truck moving over soft terrain *not only increases work output, but also reduces the likelihood of mechanical damage—often caused as a driver tries to free a bogged-down truck.*

When the excavation stage was completed and the pouring of 7 million tons of concrete (weighing more than the Great Pyramid of Egypt) that would form the 730ft Hoover Dam began, Super Duty AP Macks hauled 500 sacks of cement—48,000lb to a load—up a 26 to 30 percent grade. While the concrete was being poured, work went on day and night—holidays included—without rest for two years. Had the Super-Duty Macks failed during this crucial period, bringing the cement work to a halt, the dam's strength would have been compromised and the project aborted, but built-in Mack ruggedness kept the trucks moving hour after hour, day after day.

The AP also served as a chassis for Mack fire apparatus through 1938. As historically significant as the AP Series is, its production total is small, numbering only 285.

Probably the most famous construction project built with the help of Mack Super Duty AP Series trucks is the Hoover Dam. A fleet of over 20 big Macks, including a dozen four wheeler APs specially built for the project with 14 yard rock bodies, helped move mountains of rock on a schedule that called for the equipment to work in continuous operation 24 hours a day. Mack Museum

Chapter 5

Mack's First B Series

By the late 1920s, truck haulage was shifting from short-run, local transport to long-distance, inter-city shipping. This change in truck was the result of two developments: better roads and pneumatic tires. Recognizing the need for a higher-powered, higher-speed truck line to fit the nation's long-distance trucking needs, in the summer of 1928 Mack began development of its first B Series. The first of the new B line was a 2-4-ton model called the BJ. (Later, in 1931, the BJ's load capacity was boosted to 5-8 tons.) Also in 1928 Mack brought out a light-duty, fast delivery model called the BB. This truck carried a load rating of 1-1/2 tons and was equipped with Mack's four-cylinder 4-1/2x5 engine, also used in the AB, which produced 56hp from 283.7ci. Historians credit the BB as the first truck to be fitted with a hypoid-type rear differential. Most lighter-duty trucks of the time used a worm gear for the rear drive mechanism.

The cab and front sheet metal on these early B trucks followed truck styling of the time. The cab design progressed from a high, boxy shape with a two-piece windshield on the early B models to a lower-looking single-piece windshield style that resembled the cabs on other medium-duty trucks of the early 1930s. Both cab designs featured dual beltline moldings that extended from the cowl around the sides and back of the cab and ventilation openings in the side cowl panels, which provided a flow of fresh air to cool the driver on hot days. The gas tank was placed under the seat with the filler neck and gauge on the right side of the cab. The single-piece windshield style closely resembled the enclosed cab used on International trucks, called the A line, of the same period.

Although Mack advertising claimed it difficult to find a closed cab that offered greater comfort, with more convenience and pleasing appointments than offered on its B Series, in actual fact, these cabs with their metal door linings, wooden floorboards, and rudimentary instrumentation were exceedingly Spartan in both appearance and appointments. However, for distance truck operators there's no denying that an enclosed cab offered greater comfort than the open cabs of the earlier Mack models. Mack sales literature also mentions a deluxe cab, which differed from the standard version by the addition of extra insulation. Presumably this deluxe cab shielded the driver from some of the truck's noise.

The B line's most distinguishing appearance feature is its bold, brightmetal-plated radiator grille. The upper tank area carried the Mack emblem, and the famous Mack bulldog stood proudly on the radiator cap. Mack's F models also made use of this radiator grille, though on these trucks the radiator casing is usually painted rather than brightmetal-plated.

Mack built its BB model—often referred to as the "Baby Brother" rather than "Baby Mack," which is a name no longer used but still reserved for the smaller AB models—on a 165-1/2in wheelbase. A 177-1/2in wheelbase could be special ordered at extra cost. Even though a lighter-duty model, the BB was equipped with Mack's rubber shock absorbing spring blocks and a counter-weighted, case-hardened, drop-forged crankshaft. No Mack truck could ever be accused of not being capable of the work it was asked to do.

The next model up from the BB was the BC, which carried significant upgrades: a 3-3/4x5-1/2in 60hp engine that produced 85hp at 2000rpm, and a dual reduction rear end. The BC could be fitted with either a C cab or the enclosed cab which Mack called a "coupe type." BC models could be ordered with a 154in or 172in wheelbase and, like the BB, were fitted with a four-speed transmission.

The BF with a load rating of 2-1/2 to 4 tons entered the B Series line-up in 1932. The Mack sales literature described this six-cylinder truck as providing "fast, economical highway service." Although the BF borrowed its 65hp 3-5/8x5in engine from the BG

model, it shared the BB hypoid gear rear end. A heavier-duty BF model was also available that used a 3-7/8x5in 100hp engine and Mack's dual reduction rear. The BF was built in 156in or 174in wheelbase versions, with 192in or 210in wheelbase models available on special order. These trucks could be fitted with a five-speed transmission.

The BG, which carried a 1-1/2-ton load rating but was fitted with a more powerful 75hp engine, appeared in 1929 as a replacement for the BB. Mack advertised the BG as a fast delivery truck that could be fitted with platform, panel, or other special bodies on two chassis lengths: 156in and 168in. A tractor version was also built. The BG shared the BF's six-cylinder engine which the sales brochures rated at 70hp.

The BJ, also mentioned earlier, was a heavier-duty, high-powered truck. Despite its dual reduction rear axle and 3-4-ton capacity, Mack did not recommend this model for dump truck use.

Those wanting a chassis suited to a panel delivery body might also select the BL, a lighter-capacity six-cylinder truck with a 3-1/2x5in engine rated at 58hp. Stake and express bodies were also fitted to the BL chassis.

The three final models—the BM, BQ, and BX—were all introduced in 1932. The BM, which Mack intended as a medium-capacity truck, was fitted with a 4x5-1/2in six-cylinder engine rated at 93hp. This truck, which had a load rating of 3-5 tons, featured a dual reduction rear axle and was available in 157in or 181in wheelbase versions.

The BQ and BX formed the heavy-duty extension of the B line. Of the two, the BQ was the largest with a 6-8-ton rating. Equipped with a 128hp six-cylinder engine, dual reduction rear axle, and four-speed amidships transmission, this model was described by Mack sales literature as a "heavy-duty highway freighter and long distance high-safe-speed-schedule-clipper" (quite a mouthful of praise). BQ models were capable of 40mph speeds, loaded. For construction, mining, or shorthaul use, the BQ could also be fitted with chain drive.

The BX also gave buyers the choice of shaft or chain drive. With shaft drive, the BX had a gross weight rating of 36,000lbs. The chain drive version boosted the gross weight rating to 40,000lbs. With a 105hp 4-1/2x5in engine and vacuum-boosted brakes, the BX was well suited to long-distance freight transport as well as dump truck service. One of the dis-

Mack's B Series trucks used two different cab designs. Early trucks are most easily recognized by the taller cab with its two-piece windshield. The model BB shown here, carried the lightest load rating and was referred to as the "Baby Brother." Mack Museum

B models built from the 1930s onward used a lower-profile cab as seen on this 1936 BG flatbed.

The B line's most distinguishing feature is its bold, brightmetal-plated radiator. The upper tank carried the Mack emblem and the famous Mack Bulldog stood proudly on the radiator cap.

tinctive appearance features of this model was the door ventilators in the hood. Also, the front axle set farther back for better weight distribution. For off-road work, a C cab was available, while most trucks intended for highway use were fitted with Mack's enclosed "coupe" cab. A six-wheel model, equipped with the 4-1/2x5-1/2in (467.9ci) CF engine rated at 117hp, was also available for heavier work. Thanks to the use of Mack's patented Power Divider, all wheels on the six-wheeler's bogie were drive wheels.

Mack had experimented with six-wheel trucks as early as 1927, using a Krohn Compensator to provide the necessary wheel slippage for the four-wheel bogie. With the Power Divider, described more thoroughly in the AP chapter, Mack was able not only to power all four wheels of the rear-drive bogie, but also to direct power to the wheels having the most traction: a very beneficial concept, particularly on trucks working in uneven and loose terrain. Mack equipped the six-wheel BX with air brakes. Dump bodies up to 10cu-yd could be specified for the BX six-wheeler chassis. Whether buyers recognized the fact, with the BX six-wheeler, Mack had finally created a replacement for the AC.

As has already been mentioned, some of the B models were available as tractors for pulling semitrailers. The use of semitrailers for hauling large loads over longer distances began shortly after World War I; but semitrailer transport was slow to catch on for several reasons. Trains still handled nearly all of America's distance freight; roads were primitive at best; solid rubber-tired trucks were not suited to distance transport; and early "speed" trucks were built in the light- to medium-duty range. Trucks mainly moved freshly manufactured goods from factory to warehouse, made deliveries, and moved goods from rail terminal to local destination.

With the expansion of paved highways, the introduction of pneumatic tires, and the development of more powerful six-cylinder engines, plus changes in laws regulating truck size and weight, trucks slowly began to compete with railroads in the distance transport arena and the tractor/semitrailer combination

began to increase in popularity. Prior to the B Series, Mack created a relatively small number of tractors by shortening Model AB and AC chassis. However, these trucks were not well suited to over-the-road transport due to their slow speeds. With the development of six-cylinder trucks in the 1930s, Mack expanded its semitrailer tractor offerings with tractor models included in the BG, BF, BC, BM, BX, and BQ lines. Railroads were still the dominant freight carriers, but trucks had begun to close the gap.

With the B Series Mack inaugurated a letter system intended to group truck models by weight class. It would be easier for restorers and collectors if Mack had followed an alphabetic sequence with its letter designations, but the sequence is largely haphazard. For example, both the BC and BF had a beginning load rating of 2-1/2 tons; likewise the BB and BG models carried the same load ratings. Though, as mentioned earlier, the BG with its 75hp engine was a faster truck. It would have been especially helpful if the BX had been the heavy-weight model, but the BQ

With the expansion of improved highways, the introduction of pneumatic tires, and the development of more powerful six-cylinder engines, semitrailer trucks began to compete with railroads for distance transport. Mack offered semitrailer tractors in several B models.

held that distinction. Nonetheless, the letter designations are helpful in distinguishing the various models in the B Series and differentiating them not only by load capacity, but also by engine size.

As the lighter B models phased out in the mid-1930s, Mack prepared more modern-looking replacements in the lighter-duty E line. Toward the end of the 1930s, the heavier B models gave way to the L Series. Consequently, whereas the B line had established a consistent appearance for nearly all Mack shaft-drive trucks, now the company would present its truck line with not just two faces (the E and L), but three because a line of snub-nosed cabovers had also entered production.

As would be expected of a truck series that spanned the Great Depression, all models of the B Series production tallied far fewer than the longer-lived AB and AC models. But as a transition model that gave Mack trucks a more contemporary look, established the superiority of six-cylinder engines, and gave Mack a foothold in the ascending tractor/semi-trailer market, the B Series upheld Mack's reputation as a builder of quality trucks and continued Mack's technical dominance in the heavy truck field through such advances as the Power Divider and four-wheel drive bogie.

The BQ represented the largest of the B models. Trucks used in construction work, like the six-wheel BQ seen here, were often fitted with C cabs—more commonly associated with AC and F Series. Thanks to Mack's patented Power Divider, all wheels on both bogie axles were drive wheels. Mack Museum

Mack BM Lumber Hauler 1932-1941

The versatile, six-cylinder-powered BM became one of
Mack's largest production B models.

Chapter 6

Mack Gets a New Light-Duty Line

lthough Mack benefited from public works contracts during the depression, to say that truck
sales were dismal would be an overstatement.
But it wasn't just Mack that was hurting. Every car
and truck maker had its back against the wall—bank-

ruptcies were claiming some of the most esteemed
manufacturers. In this economic climate, companies—like individuals—turned to each other for help.
In 1932, Willys and International Harvester struck a
deal whereby IH would sell the newly designed

*In 1934 Mack signed an agreement with Reo to rebadge
and mildly restyle that company's light and medium duty
trucks as Mack Jr. models. The new Mack Jr. line appeared in 1936. Two models were offered: a pickup (seen
here) and a panel delivery truck. Both shared styling and
chassis components with Reo's car line.*

Early Reo-built Mack Jr. pickups are extremely rare. This 1936 example, owned by Richard Sherker, is one of only five in existence. Reportedly, only twenty-seven were built.

Willys C-1 pickup and panel truck under the International nameplate. Although the new light-duty models didn't bear much resemblance to the existing medium-duty IH line, dealership traffic increased. When International unveiled its new C-line trucks in 1934, their own half-ton models (powered by the Willys engine) stood prominently in the line-up.

Mack also eyed the sales that could be generated by a lighter-duty line and reached an agreement in October 1934 with Reo to rebadge and mildly restyle (grille shells were different) that company's light- and medium-duty trucks as Mack Jr.'s. For Mack, the Reo connection gave what today is called "full market penetration," but during the depression, having more models to sell went by a simpler expression— namely "survival." The link with Reo was a good one in that the Lansing, Michigan, company also adhered to sound engineering and had built a reputation for dependability and speed in its Reo Speedwagon 1-ton to 1-1/2-ton trucks, which had also gained both glamour and notoriety from their widespread use by Prohibition-era rum runners.

The Mack Jr. models appeared in 1936 and consisted of trucks in the 1/2-ton to 3-ton range. Mack identified the 1/2-ton Mack Jr. as the 1M. A pickup and panel delivery were offered, both based on a Reo sedan chassis. The larger models consisted of the 1-1/2-ton 10M, a 2-ton 20M, and a 3-ton 30M. A COE (cab-over-engine) version of the 30M was also offered, called the 30MT. The T stood for "Traffic," a reference to the truck's shorter overall length that made it more maneuverable for city deliveries.

For 1937, Mack added the 2M, a rebadged version of Reo's new Speed Delivery truck. Like Reo, Mack offered the 2M with either a four-cylinder or six-cylinder engine. Each was available on a short (114in) or long (120in) wheelbase. Mack called the four-cylinder, short wheelbase model the 2M4A. The four-cylinder engined truck with the long wheelbase was designated the 2M4B. The short and long wheelbase versions with the six-cylinder engine were called the 2M6A and 2M6B respectively. The shorter wheelbase trucks carried a 6ft box while the longer wheelbase models were fitted with a 7ft box. All four engine and wheelbase combinations could be rated at either 1/2-ton or 3/4-ton capacities. The 3/4-ton version, designated by an S (as in 2M4AS) had a heavier-duty rear axle and oversize 6.50x16 tires.

The Reo Speed Delivery and Mack Jr. were identical in nearly all respects except for nameplates. Mack, of course, attached its familiar bulldog mascot to the top of the grille and wrapped two horizontal bars from the grille around the sides of the hood. These trim bars interrupted the Reo's "waterfall" frontal appearance and cluttered a good design. As with the previous (1936) 1/2-ton offerings, the Speed Delivery (or Mack 2M) was built both as a pickup and a panel truck. Mack literature does not show the station wagon Speed Delivery model that appears in the Reo catalogs. Imagine what a sought-after truck a Mack "woody wagon" would be!

The Reo link-up proved a success with Mack sales jumping spectacularly in 1936, topping 4,000 units for the first time since 1930. Attributing sales in part to the broader market offerings, Mack moved quickly to design and tool up production for its own light-duty line, which joined Mack's new E Series in 1938. Since introduction of the light-duty (this term has to be used advisedly since nothing Mack ever built is truly "light-duty"), E Series trucks overlapped with the Reo-built Mack Jr. It's likely that some Mack dealers had both Reo-built Mack 2Ms and the new Mack-built ED model light trucks on their lots at the same time. Now there's a dilemma: is a Mack a Mack if its not Mack through and through? As we'll see soon, nothing is built like a Mack, even when the truck has a light-duty rating.

With the possible exception of the Diamond T model 204, Mack's ED Series were the most rugged trucks ever offered in the so-called "light-duty" field. Even the legendary Dodge Power Wagon doesn't come close! Mack sales literature got the new ED models' personality right with the slogan, "Bringing real truck stamina and dependability to the light delivery field." Like the Mack Jr., the ED was offered in two wheelbases. On the ED, however, the standard wheelbase measured 120-1/2in, which compares to

In 1937, Reo restyled its pickups and panels, giving the new line more of a truck look. The Mack-badged versions are readily identified by the bulldog bounding up from the top of the grille, Mack Jr. nameplates on the sides of the hood, and the Mack script in the center of the hubcaps. Two brightmetal strips wrapping around the front of the grille mark the most noticeable appearance difference.

The Reo-supplied 2M pickups and panels that came in short and long wheelbase versions and were offered with either a four- or six-cylinder engine. The 2M panel deliv- *ery's no-nonsense styling seems to make it a closer member of the Mack family than its 1M predecessor.*

120in for the long wheelbase Mack Jr., while the extended (Special) model used a 136-1/2in wheelbase. The ED's six-cylinder 3-3/16x4-3/8in L-head engine, also built by Continental, displaced 210ci, so it was just slightly larger than the Mark Jr. engine (at 209ci.), but at 67hp it was also slightly less powerful. The Mack Jr. engine had a rated output of 72hp. The ED engine may have been a few horsepower shy of the Mack Jr., but it was a quality power plant through and through. With thirty-three studs to hold down the head, an owner wasn't likely to experience

head warpage or a leaking head gasket, and hardened exhaust valves and seats meant there wouldn't be any need to pull the head for a valve job—at least not for 100,000 miles. Should a buyer worry over the ED's five fewer horsepower, an optional four-speed transmission, not available on the Mack Jr., and rear axle ratios as low as 6.333:1 made up for any power deficiency.

Mack styled its light-duty ED trucks to match the larger E Series models. Prominent features included a one-piece windshield (Mack Jr.'s had a two-piece V'd windshield) and high-crowned, cycle-style fenders that looked similar to those used on the bigger E Series trucks. The boss-truck parentage could also be found underneath, starting with a beefy frame constructed of 7in deep, 3-1/6in thick side channels and four cross members—three boxed and one channel type. At the rear, the ED featured Mack's exclusive rubber, shock-insulating spring mounts. As would be expected, Mack's own light truck was in reality a scaled-down big truck.

In standard form, the ED Model lacked the chromed grille, front bumper and hubcaps of the Mack Jr., making it plainer than pickups from most other manufacturers. But then, Mack wasn't selling its trucks on looks—although overall Mack styling has always been elegant in a chiseled granite sort of way. Chrome-plated trim could be ordered as extra cost equipment and a deluxe cab with a dome light, ash tray, cigar lighter, door arm rest and coat hooks was also available. ED models were sold as a stripped chassis, with a list price of $675. Starting with this basic chassis, buyers could build one of several trucks: a "retailer" cabover style delivery van

that looked very much like International's Metro, a standard delivery, the pickup cab plus a variety of utility bodies, the pickup cab and box, or pickup cab and express or stake bodies.

Mack built the ED through 1944, although production after 1941 went to the military in the form of fire pumpers built on the stripped chassis. Production never topped 1,000 units in a calendar year and Mack didn't resume the ED Series (or introduce another light-duty series) after the war. ED Production by year was 152 in 1938; 704 in 1939; 589 in 1940; 707 in 1941; 274 in 1942; 0 in 1943; and 260 in 1944.

Mack introduced the first of the new E line models in 1936, the same year Mack began marketing Reo-built trucks in its light-duty range. It seems clear that the Reo deal was intended only as a stop-gap measure to give Mack a reliable line of light-duty trucks, because the E line would soon be expanded to fill Mack's light-duty gap. The first E models to appear were of a new "cabover" design, which eliminated the hood by placing the cab over the engine (hence the "cabover" name). This new cabover, also called Traffic Type, design offered numerous advan-

A 1937 Mack Jr. ad.

tages for trucks operated primarily inside cities. Mounting the cab over the engine gave the driver a tall perch from which to view oncoming traffic; the driver's position at the very front of the truck eliminated the obstruction caused by the hood and front fenders. The cabover or Traffic Type design also gave this style of truck a 3ft shorter overall length when compared with conventional models, which enabled a much shorter turning radius and greater maneuverability—definite pluses for city operation. The weight distribution of these cabover models hit a perfect balance with one-third of the truck's weight resting on the front axle and two-thirds on the rear. This one-third front, two-thirds rear axle weight distribution conforms exactly with the tire configuration—the front axle carries single tires while the rear carries dual tires. Finally the cabover design gave maximum usable body space with limited overall length.

These E cabovers are dead ringers for the Mack C Series Traffic Types and the two are easily confused. The major difference, besides a slight repositioning of the grille, is in the load capacity: E models having more moderate duty ratings. These E Series cabovers with Traffic Type styling came in two models: the EC and EB.

The first of the E Series trucks in the traditional long-nose configuration also appeared in 1936. This was the EH, a handsome looking truck in the medium-duty range. This new conventional model contained many advanced styling features that would continue to be seen on Mack's lighter- and medium-duty trucks into the 1950s. Among the more prominent of these were cycle-style front fenders along with the chrome plating in the grille and a sloping, single-piece windshield. (International adopted similar cycle-style front fenders on its D Series trucks, first introduced in 1937, and continued this fender

As the only styling difference, the horizontal bars across the hood of the Mack 2M obstructed the simple "waterfall" grille and cluttered an otherwise clean design.

In 1938 Mack introduced its own "home built" pickup, called the ED. With the possible exception of the Diamond T model 204, the Mack ED is the most overbuilt truck ever sold in the light duty field.

design on the heavier-duty K and KB models through 1949.) The EH used the EN310 six-cylinder engine from the former BG model and had a GVW (gross vehicle weight) rating of 19,500lbs. Mack also built a lighter EH model rated at 18,000lb GVW. Mack also built two lighter-duty E models above the ED pickup. These were the EE, a 12,000lb GVW truck equipped with a 75hp 253ci engine, and the EF, a slightly beefier 14,000lb GVW truck equipped with a 9 hp 290ci engine.

All conventional E types share the same cab with its one-piece windshield and distinctive double belt-line molding that began on the cowl just in front of the windshield pillars and ran across the doors and around the back of the cab. Although the interior is rather sparse, a glovebox on the passenger side of the

dash gives a symmetrical balance to a similarly shaped instrument panel on the driver's side.

Along with attractive styling, the E Series presented several mechanical advances. Hydraulic brakes were installed on all models for fast, sure stopping even when fully loaded. Steering was also made safer and surer by the adoption of Mack's "Archemoid" steering mechanism. The Mack-exclusive Archemoid steering gear replaced the worm and sector mechanism typically used in car and truck steering boxes or the era with a much more rugged steering mechanism of Mack design. While the Archemoid steering follows the basic worm and sector layout, it employs a much larger sector gear for greater mechanical advantage in the steering process and to reduce wear and possibility of breakage.

EO938

As replacements for the antiquated AB Series, the up-to-date conventional style E models reestablished Mack as strong player in the medium duty field

Left
A look at the ED chassis shows that this pickup's Mack heritage is more than skin deep. The rugged frame is constructed of side channels that measure a full 7in deep in their center sections and four sturdy cross-members. Note that the three rear cross-members shown are boxed—that is, enclosed on all four sides.

The E Series included a wide range of models with load ranges from 12,000lb to 23,000lb GVW. This E model saw service as a water tanker for a fire department.

While Mack E Series trucks came standard-equipped with five-speed transmissions, some of the larger models (including the EQ) were available with a ten-speed monoshift transmission. As the name implies, the monoshift used a single lever to shift all ten forward speeds—a feature that made for easier shifting and less driver fatigue.

In 1937, the conventional E Series trucks expanded with new models in the 16,000lb to 23,000lb GVW range. Besides the EH already mentioned, these included the EG, rated at 16,000lb GVW and equipped with a 271ci engine and four-speed transmission; the EG and EJ, both rated at 16,000lb GVW; the EM, rated at 23,400lb GVW, also equipped with the EN 310 engine and five-speed transmission; and the EH, a 19,500lb GVW truck also fitted with the EN 310/five-speed transmission combination. The differences in the EG and EJ trucks were in the engine, the EG having a 108hp 330ci engine while the EJ used a smaller 288ci engine.

Also in 1937, a new line of cabover models joined the E Series. These trucks with their short stub nose are not to be confused with early flat-front Traffic Type trucks. The styling and design features of these revised cabover models are closer to Ford's medium-duty cabover trucks of the late 1930s, early 1940s vintage than to any of Mack's earlier Traffic Types. More prominent styling features of these later E Series cabovers include the short nose fronted by the pouncing Bulldog and distinctive E line grille, removeable side hood covers, and front hinged doors. The stubby hood allowed the engine to be positioned

E Series trucks are powered by L-6 gasoline engines in a variety of displacements. Mack also used the E models to introduce the idea of diesel power in its medium duty trucks.

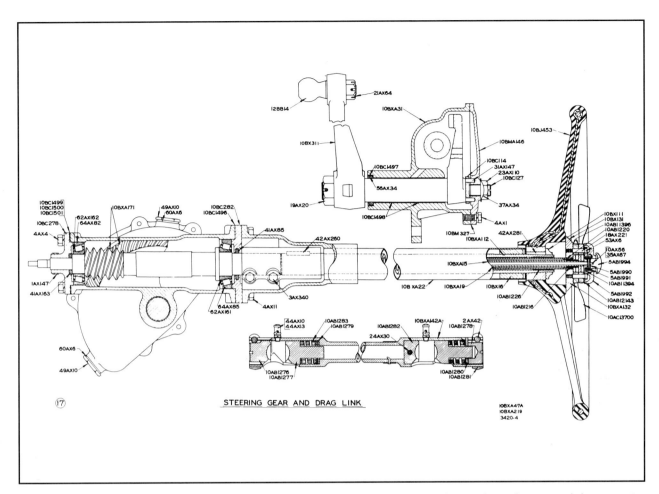

STEERING GEAR AND DRAG LINK

With the E Series, the Mack-exclusive Archemoid steering gear replaced the worm and sector mechanism typically used in car and truck steering boxes of the era with a much more rugged steering mechanism of Mack design. While the Archemoid steering follows the basic worm and sector layout, it employs a much larger sector gear for greater mechanical advantage in the steering process and to reduce wear and possibility of breakage.
Mack Museum

ahead of the seats, reducing the size of the "dog house"—an appropriately descriptive name for the engine cover. The removeable side hood covers, along with the engine's more forward location, made service far easier than on Traffic Types where routine maintenance had to be performed from inside the cab. Drivers appreciated the front-hinged doors that give better visibility when backing the truck into tight spaces than the rear-hinged doors used with the earlier Traffic Types.

The stub-nosed cabover came in six models: the EEU and EHU, both rated at 12,000lb GVW; the EFU and EMU, rated at 14,000lb GVW; and the EGU and EQU, rated at 16,000lb GVW. Differences between models with the same load rating were in engine size. While the EEU, EFU, and EGU models were fitted with smaller engines having bore and stroke measurements of 3-1/2x4-3/8in for the EEU, 3-5/8x4-3/8in for the EFU, and 3-3/4x4-7/8in for the EGU, the EHU, EMU, and EQU all worked with a larger 3-5/8x5in engine. An EHU model with a 19,500lb GVW rating was also offered. Prices on these trucks ranged from $3600 for the 12,000lb load range models to $5150 for the 16,000lb models—quite substantial figures given the deflated economy of the times.

With the Mack's new E Series now covering the full medium-duty range, the AB model, which had been in production since 1914, could finally be phased out. The last AB, carrying a 20,000lb GVW rating, was replaced by the ER, also rated at 20,000lbs and fitted with chain drive. An FM gear drive model, rated at 20,000lbs GVW, was also offered. In the spring of 1937, Mack broadened the E Series still further with the EQ, rated at 23,400lbs and fitted with Mack's EN 354 gasoline engine. By the end of 1938, the EM and ES joined the E Series line-up. The ES is an oddity in the shaft-drive E line in that it matched the specifications of the EQ, but used chain drive. With the E line in place, Mack discontinued its sales agreement with Reo and the Mack Jr. became history.

Along with the cabovers and conventional trucks, Mack also adapted the E Series to semitrailer tractors, which were designated by a "T" added to the letters indicating the model. Mack built E Series semi tractors in EFT, EHT, EMT models, the second letter indicating the load rating. The EFT used the EN 290 engine (same as the EF conventional) while the EHT used the EN310 and the EMT the EN 354. All three trucks were fitted with five-speed transmissions. The larger engines helped better suit these trucks to distance hauling, which was the primary service of tractor/trailer units.

In 1937, a new line of cabover models joined the E Series. These trucks with their short stubby hood placed the engine ahead of the seats. The removable side hood covers, along with the engine's more forward location, made ser- *vice far easier than on Traffic Types where routine maintenance had to be performed from inside the cab. Mack Museum*

Besides its configuration as a tractor model, note that this truck also uses chain drive. Mack offered chain drive as an alternative to gear drive in some of the heavier duty E models.

Sales were strongest among the heavier duty E models. Note that this EH dump has been fitted with a front drive axle.

The EQ with its 23,400lb load rating marked the top of the E line. This truck, also fitted with a front drive axle, carries a Quick-Way shovel.

With America beginning to climb out of the depression at the eve of World War II, Mack truck production was topping 10,000 units a year, making it the nation's largest builder of heavy-duty trucks. Now that the AB and AC had been phased out along with the B Series trucks, the E models accounted for the bulk of this sales success, with the medium-duty EH model proving to be the most popular.

As the United States watched Europe careen toward war, the Army placed an order with Mack for military trucks suited to troop transport. The largest segment of this order, 368 trucks, was comprised of model EEU cabover types modified for military use. Also included in the order were 80 EE models fitted with dump bodies.

After the war, Mack continued to build most of the medium-duty E models, but the lighter trucks in this series were discontinued. As a result, the 12,000lb GVW EE model was the lightest-duty truck in the Mack line-up during the early post-World War II period. The postwar E models remained in production through 1950 when Mack introduced its new A Series medium-duty truck line. The cabover E models also ceased production in 1950, leaving Mack without a COE type truck for over a year. Apparently seeing the need for a medium-duty COE, Mack reissued the EFU snub-nose in 1951 as the A20U. This truck remained in production for just two years.

E Series Macks also saw use as fire apparatus. A community that purchased one of these smaller fire trucks was showing its pride in itself and its fire department by purchasing a Mack since the capacity of an E Series fire apparatus could also be obtained from fire apparatus mounted on Chevrolet, Ford, Dodge, or International truck chassis. With a 500gal per minute pumping capacity, type 45 E Series District Pumpers were best suited to smaller communities.

Picking up sales in another direction, Mack built a lengthened E chassis as a school bus platform. Both EH and EJ models were used. Although very few E Series bus chassis were sold—EH bus sales totaled 53 while the EJ bus total reached only 38—here again buyers benefited from Mack's high quality engineering and resulting durability. However, given the cost premium of a Mack truck, few school boards would have been able to justify the added expense of a Mack bus over a bus mounted on a Ford, Chevy, or International chassis, particularly in rural areas where few tax payers felt prosperous enough to purchase a medium-duty E Series Mack over a truck of a less expensive make.

In 1949, just before the E Series bowed out to its replacement, the new A line, Mack used the E models to introduce the idea of diesel power in medium-duty trucks. (Mack had begun using diesel engines in its heaviest-duty trucks in the late 1930s.) To publicize the new engine and to introduce the new diesel engine to Mack service personnel as well as potential buyers, Mack set up a diesel caravan road show comprised of a specially painted EH tractor and trailer that contained a display of the new 672 diesel engines. A team of specially trained technicians traveled with the caravan, giving demonstrations on the diesel's advantages at selected locations. The display toured the country for seven-and-one-half months. The EH semi-tractor pulling the diesel display was powered with the new engine, which was indicated

Mack continued to build the heavier duty EH and EQ models after the war

B Series Mack Jr.

If Mack had decided to build a light truck in the post-war years, most likely it would have looked like George Sprowl, Sr.'s miniature B model. To build his "Baby Mack," George started with a junked 1956 B30 and a burned-out 1983 Ford F350 with only 21,000 miles.

The Mack cab was narrowed 5in and channeled 3in. The Mack front fenders were also sectioned to reduce their overall dimensions but keep them proportionally accurate with the big trucks. Mack air ride suspension was transferred to the Ford front end. To give the truck a Mack feel, Sprowl installed a 105hp Cummins 4BT diesel. The box is a Dodge step side because the rounded fenders look like they belong on a B Mack. And the tailgate even reads M-A-C-K.

The little Mack turns heads wherever it travels.

by the Mack Diesel nameplates attached to the sides of the hood.

Although the relatively light-duty EE model had continued in production to 1950, when the new A Series appeared, Mack eliminated trucks in the under 17,000lb GVW class. The EF lived on into 1951, at which point the E Series' replacement was completed.

At the point the E Series had entered Mack's truck line-up, the company was building a whole spectrum of models from the CJ (Traffic type), to the mighty BX, to the E Series, and even the Bulldog-appearing AK. With the E Series, Mack had begun to consolidate its truck models into two lines—the lighter and medium-duty in one grouping and the heavier and off-road trucks in another. Now with the appearance of the A line (and continuation of some of the larger L models), this consolidation was essentially complete. Mack's E Series had been instrumen-

E Series Macks also saw use as fire apparatus. A volunteer fire department could take great pride in its E Series

With a 500gpm pumping capacity, type 45 E Series District Pumpers were best suited to smaller communities.

tal in dramatically upgrading the styling—something particularly needed with the lighter-duty models where sales were made on appearance as well as toughness and mechanical integrity. With their higher sales volume, all of Mack's major medium-duty competitors—Ford, Chevrolet, Dodge and International—were able to give their trucks frequent styling updates. To compete in this arena Mack needed to establish a "classic" look that was free of the styling gimmicks of the moment. The E Series accomplished that goal, as did the 1950s and 1960s B Series, and to a lesser extent the A Series.

It goes without saying that an E model Mack makes a very handsome and desirable collector truck. Production was largest for the EE, EF, EH, and EQ models. Probably the most highly desirable of all the E models are the pickups—here we are talking about a very low production model with only 2,686 total units built. Of course, the collector status of the pickup comes not just from its low production and appealing styling, but also from its uniqueness in the line-up of a company famous for its heavy-hitters.

In 1949, just before the E Series bowed out to its replacement, the new A line, Mack used the E models to introduce diesel power in medium duty trucks. A diesel powered EQT is seen here hauling a load of new 1950 Hudsons. Note the tractor's long wheel base, allowing two more cars to be added to the load. Mack Museum

Chapter 7

F Series Super-Duty Macks

Having earned a reputation for ruggedness and durability with its six-wheeler AC and AP-6s, Mack wasn't about to abandon the super-duty truck market when its Bulldog models finally phased out of production. Consequently, in 1937 a new super-duty line, called the F Series, emerged as the

Needing a chassis that could be equipped with either diesel or gasoline powerplants, Mack introduced the F series in 1937 as the replacement to its recently phased out AC and AP models. The truck shown here was owned and restored by the late Grover Swank, a friend who provided research information for this book. Photo courtesy Grover Swank

F models can be identified by a combination of the BG radiator and hood and the C cab with half doors. The truck shown here is a 1939 FN dump.

heavy capacity AC and AP's replacement. The timing was right for engineering a new super-duty line. Diesel engines were becoming available for trucks and Mack needed a chassis that could be equipped with either diesel or gasoline powerplants.

Although in the mid-1930s, truck operators still had to be sold on the advantages of diesel power, the greater operating economy of a diesel engine soon spoke for itself. Had it not been for the interruption of civilian truck development caused by World War II, diesel engines probably would have overrun the heavy-duty truck market within a decade. As it was, diesel power began to see widespread acceptance in the 1950s.

From a styling point of view, the new F models used the BG radiator and hood and a C-type cab with half doors. (The driver could be protected in the winter by enclosing the cab with canvas side curtains.) As would be expected of a truck line designed for heavy service, chassis construction on an F Series Mack is extremely rugged. A close look at frame of an F model Mack shows that these trucks are actually built with two frames—two separate pieces of channel steel, one set inside the other, make up the side channels. On some models triple-thickness frames were fitted at extra cost. As with previous heavy-duty Mack models, the F Series used chain drive.

As the F line was phased into production through 1937 and 1938, several models were introduced in the 35,000lb to 50,000lb GVW range. By 1938, the F Series lineup consisted of the FG, 35,000lb GVW; FH and FJ, 45,000lb GVW; and the FK, 50,000lb GVW; plus two super-duty, special permit vehicles, the FC 6 tractor, which could haul trailers with 100,000lb (50-ton) loads, and the FCSW, which could carry loads of 30 tons or more. The FCSW—in Mack nomenclature SW indicates six-wheel models—is the first Mack to use an offset cab.

The FP model, introduced in 1941, replaced the ER and ES trucks from the E. Some juggling also occurred at the bottom of the F Series: production ceased on the FG in 1942 at the same time a similarly rated FT was added in its place. Since the F Series trademark was chain drive, like its Bulldog predecessors, only a few F models were reintroduced after World War II. Those continuing in production included the FT, upgraded with a larger engine, and the FW, which now carried a 50,000lb GVW rating. A small number of the large FC trucks were

Side curtains could be installed to protect the driver in cold or rainy weather.

also built. The postwar FT and FW trucks have a sharply different appearance than their prewar counterparts. The postwar models used an L Series cab with half doors and cycle-style fenders. There's no mistaking a postwar FT or FW for an L model; however, the chain drive and angular B-style radiator, not to mention the half doors, are clear F Series departures. The postwar FCs also used an L cab and benefited from mechanical upgrades developed on war production.

Along with diesel power, the F Series offered a five-speed transmission plus two-speed auxiliary, giving ten forward speeds. Other F Series design characteristics, besides chain drive, included a narrower frame, set-back front axle for better weight distribution, air-brakes, and Mack's unique rubber cushioning on the spring mounts to insulate the cargo and driver from road shocks. As early as 1920, Mack had devised jump tests where unloaded trucks were catapulted off ramps to study the shock effects on the suspensions and wheels as the trucks crashed back onto the ground. The jumps were recorded on film with special slow-motion movie cameras so that engineers could study the shock effects on the suspension and chassis components. Among the improvements resulting from these tests was a patented method for encapsulating the spring ends in rubber blocks that served to cushion the chassis from abrupt shocks. The Mack Rubber Shock Insulator, as the rubber-encapsulated spring mounts were called, first appeared on AB models in 1921. The rear springs on an F Series, as well as most Macks from 1921, are not secured to the axle as is the case on other trucks. Instead, they slip into rubber blocks, which sit inside rugged metal cages that attach to the axles. Since springs aren't attached to the axles, rugged A-frame design radius rods are used to hold the axles in place. On the six-wheel models the massive radius rods to the front drive axle also house shock absorbers that serve to cushion road shocks. Ball and socket couplings at the radius rods' forward ends allow up-and-down movement as well as a small amount of lateral movement with the axle. To locate the rear drive axle, six-wheel trucks also contain a third interaxle radius rod of Herculean proportions, which sits inside the springs.

Diesel power greatly boosted the F models' performance and stamina in rugged use settings and benefited the more conventional use trucks through

Mack's attention to detail shows in the company trade name in the dust covers on the wheels.

Left
A close look at the frame of an F model Mack shows that these trucks are actually built with two frames, one inside the other. As with previous heavy duty Mack models, the F Series used chain drive.

greater fuel economy. The reason most often given by cost-conscious truck buyers for choosing diesel power is the long-term economy of a diesel engine. Until the early 1970s, diesel fuel sold for a fraction of the cost of gasoline. While more recently the prices of diesel fuel and gasoline have been closer to par, diesel-engined trucks are still more economical to operate because of the greater efficiency of a diesel engine. In the late thirties when Mack introduced its first truck diesel, gasoline engines were capable of extracting about 18 to 19 percent usable energy from the fuel burned. Diesel engines, in contrast, operated at a 26 percent efficiency level. In addition, because of their more rugged design, diesels typically give much longer service. A second, significant advantage

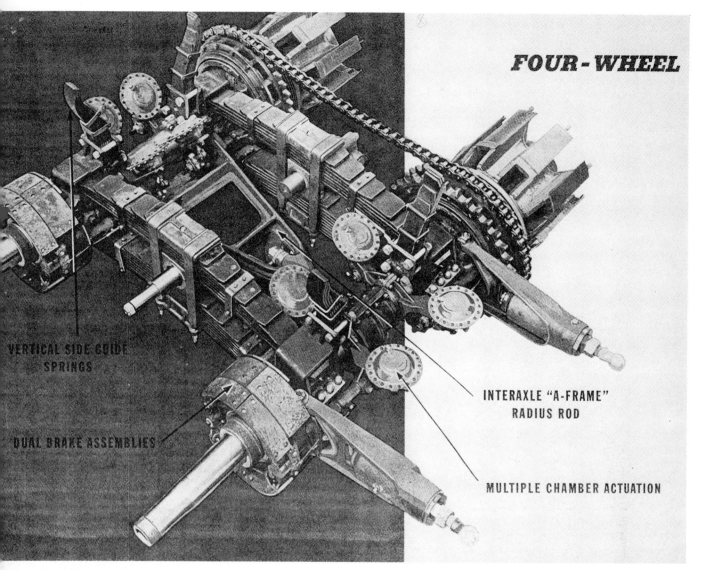

VERTICAL SIDE GUIDE SPRINGS

DUAL BRAKE ASSEMBLIES

INTERAXLE "A-FRAME" RADIUS ROD

MULTIPLE CHAMBER ACTUATION

The rear springs on F Series Macks are not secured to the axle as is the case with other trucks, but slip into rubber blocks that sit inside rugged metal cages that attach to the axles. Rugged A-frame radius rods hold the axles in place. To locate the rear drive axle, six-wheel trucks also employ a massive interaxle radius rod located inside the springs.

is the substantially increased efficiency and power of a diesel engine.

Developing a diesel engine suitable for heavy truck use posed several engineering challenges, the most significant of which was controlling the combustion process so that the intense power of the exploding fuel gases didn't slam against the pistons with such force as to destroy the engine. Mack conquered the combustion challenge by adopting a patented Lanova precombustion system. In the Lanova design, the fuel injector and a unique dual-chambered energy cell are positioned opposite one another over the combustion chamber. When the injector discharges, the spray of fuel/air mixture travels across the combustion chamber and enters the inner chamber of the energy cell. Some of the fuel mixture continues into the energy cell's outer chamber where combustion occurs. The ignited and rapidly expanding gases blast back out of the energy cell into the combustion chamber creating a high turbulence that provides thorough and complete combustion and exerts equal forces against the piston—producing a smooth and powerful combustion stroke.

Along with its own diesel, Mack also offered its larger FC with diesel engines built by Cummins and

Buda. Part of the significance of the Mack-Lanova engine is that Mack was the first independent truck maker to develop a proprietary diesel. For Mack, having its own diesel meant keeping the lion's share of its engine production in-house as well as assuring diesel truck buyers of Mack quality throughout. The Mack diesel represented years of experimentation; numerous patents were obtained covering many of its design features and making it an engine worthy of the Mack name.

A practice that Mack made quite common was basing both diesel and gasoline engines on the same block. Where this occurs, the gasoline engine has an EN (ENgine) letter prefix while the diesel has an END (ENgine Diesel) prefix to the engine number, which represents displacement. As an example, the basic block of the END 519 diesel, used in the F Se-

ries, differs from the EN 519 in that the cylinders on the diesel are sleeved. Since sleeves can also be installed in the block of a gasoline engine that has damaged cylinder walls or has been bored past acceptable tolerances, the close similarity of the basic engine castings has been a boon to rebuilders of gasoline-powered F Series trucks. The END 519 proved to be one of Mack's more successful engines, with 18,000 built for military use alone.

One might wonder why Mack stayed with chain drive for its F Series. Actually there were several reasons for keeping the "chain gang" as opposed to going with shaft drive.

On a chain-drive truck, road speed can be increased or decreased easily and quickly by installing smaller or larger front drive sprockets. On a shaft-drive truck, changing road speed would require an

Where Mack based its diesel and gasoline engines on the same block, the gasoline engine has an EN letter prefix while the diesel has an END prefix to the engine number that represents displacement.

Since they were also equipped with chain drive, F Series tractors were used for hauling equipment and other heavy trailer loads for long distance, over-the-road haul- *ing. Note the capstan and winch mounted behind the cab of these trucks.*

elaborate and expensive tear down or replacement of the rear differential. Since heavy-duty trucks may work in a variety of settings—moving earth on a construction site or carrying coal out of a quarry— that may require higher or lower gearing depending on the type of work being done, the ability to change gearing in a small amount of time makes the trucks much more versatile. Lest one think that fitting the right sprocket combination could turn an F Series truck into a real road hauler, it should be noted that Mack rated the F Series chassis at a maximum speed of 40mph.

The F Series wore its "Built like a Mack Truck" badge of distinction well, as have all Macks. F Series Macks helped build the New York World's Fair of 1939-40 and later worked in constructing the St.

Lawrence Seaway. Mining companies bought F Series Macks, particularly the super-duty FCSW models, to move earth and ore. And a number of super-duty F models went to the military for use in heavy construction work for World War II. In the late 1940s, what was then the world's largest anthracite coal strip mine located near Coaldale, Pennsylvania, purchased a fleet of 35 FCSW super-duty Macks to cut away as much as 700ft of overburden to expose a rich 80ft thick coal seam. Day and night the giant Mack dump trucks shuttled in and out of the pit, hauling 50-ton loads up 8 percent grades. Like most postwar FCSWs, the trucks in this fleet were equipped with supercharged Cummins HBDS diesel engines, which, though not without problems, had enormous power and gave good service under severe use conditions. To get an idea of the brawn of an FCSW Mack, the truck really has to be seen firsthand. But given the scarcity of these models today and the slim opportunity for seeing an FCSW "in the flesh," some sense of these trucks can be gained by realizing that the transmission weighed nearly a ton. When a FCSW Mack needed to be lifted off the ground, railroad jacks were the tool to use. A bottom rear bogie spring weighed 650lb and the top spring weighed 400lb. The bogie was actually fitted with eight springs, four on either side of the axles to support the load and two perpendicular springs at each end of the bogie to prevent the load from shifting or tipping. The chain mechanism on a four-wheel-driven Mack FCSW is also a sight to behold.

To get a sense of the brawn of an FCSW Mack, one really has to see the truck firsthand. This 1943 FCSW has been displayed at the Antique Truck Club of America's annual meet.

One of the largest Mack trucks, the FCSW's transmission weighed nearly a ton; the bottom rear bogie spring weighed 650lb; while the top spring weighed 400lb. To lift the rear of the truck off the ground, railroad jacks were the tool to use. To power the FCSW's four-wheel bogie, a pair of beefy chains run from the jackshaft to sprockets on the forward axle. Just outboard of the main drive sprocket are another set of sprockets driving the chains to the rear axle. This mechanism is a sight to behold.

To power the four-wheel-drive bogie, a pair of beefy chains run from the jackshaft to sprockets on the forward axle. Just outboard of the main drive sprocket are another set of sprockets driving the chains to the rear axle. These chains run from the forward to the rear axle sprockets, looping over an idler gear that helps control chain tension on their return. In the brutal work of open pit mining, chain wear was often rapid and mechanics became adept at replacing chains where they broke, which often meant lying on their backs in mud.

Braking for the super-duty FCSW was handled by dual brake assemblies on each of the four wheels, plus the single brake assemblies on the front wheels. As mentioned earlier, brakes on the big F Series models were powered by compressed air. Dual brake assemblies does not mean two sets of shoes on each axle, but rather two separate sets of shoes at each wheel. To support their enormous payloads, the frames on these trucks had a 12in drop and weighed 50lb-ft. A vacuum-boosted clutch and hydraulic-assisted steering enabled drivers to put these trucks though their paces for eight-hour shifts or longer without collapsing of fatigue.

For massive ruggedness, nothing beats a super-duty F Series Mack. In the same duty range as the FCSW, Mack also built a truck tractor capable of hauling 50-ton trailers. Although most of the F models disappeared when civilian truck production ceased in 1942, Mack revived the 35,000lb GVW FT for a short period after World War II and an FW model replaced the prewar FK. The super-duty FC models also remained in production through 1947. A few styling changes distinguish the postwar F mod-els. Although the B radiator and hood are retained, the cab is from the L Series, but with half doors. For weather protection, side curtains were provided.

The almost legendary reputation Mack's F mod-els garnered for themselves in the most rugged working settings far outweighs their significance from a sales perspective since fewer than 2,000 were built. Today the most popular are the FCs, particu-larly six-wheeler tractors. No truck show is complete without a couple of these beasts in the lineup. The sight to see, however, is the king of the F Series—the brutally awesome FSCW.

Note the chain oil dispenser mounted above the jackshaft. Instructions on the dispenser container say "fill daily." FCSW trucks were used exclusively off-road in conditions where chain wear could be rapid.

A modern CL Series Mack helps put the FCSW's size in perspective.

Chapter 8

C Series Traffic Types

n the 1920s, Mack had focused on building strong trucks. In the 1930s, without losing sight of the importance of strength and durability, a new emphasis emerged. Driven by the pressures of a shrinking market caused by the economic contraction of the depression, Mack sought to develop a greater variety of trucks for different uses. This diversity of models would lead Mack into a brief presence in the pickup field, as well as a short marketing "marriage" with REO to field a line of lighter-duty models as well as pickups. Besides these ventures, Mack would also develop new models that hit the target of trucking's future. The success stories were, of course, the semitrailer tractor and the stub-nosed "Traffic Types."

Since the development of Mack's trailer models is told in the 1930s B Series chapter and elsewhere, this discussion will focus on the all-new Traffic Types. The rapid expansion of paved highways was creating a new industry in long-distance trucking at the same time an increase in commerce was also expanding short haul, inner city trucking. The narrow streets and alleys in which this inner city commerce moved called for a new truck design that allowed tighter turning radius. The way to give any vehicle a tighter turning radius is to reduce its overall length. Of course nothing would be gained by reducing the length of the cargo area, so Mack's engineers concentrated on reducing the truck's frontal area. The result, which first appeared in 1933, was an all-new truck style called the "Traffic Type."

The new Traffic Type came in two models: the CH and CJ. Both shared a "pug nose" appearance that resulted from a very short hood and blunt B Series style radiator. The tall cab construction on these trucks resulted from the engine's being stuffed partly inside, but mostly under the cab. Other distinctive features of Mack's early Traffic Types included an unusually large, two-piece windshield and windows in the front cab corners ahead of the doors, which

combined with the expansive windshield area and high seating position of the driver to give excellent forward visibility. The set-back cab doors hinged in the normal forward location so the driver climbed into the cab by mounting steps attached to the back of the front fender. On later Traffic Types the doors hinged at the rear and the driver entered the cab from a step attached to the front of the fender. As any experienced trucker knows, front hinged doors make for better visibility when backing the truck since if need be the driver can open the door and look around the side of the truck to check for clearance and obstacles. However, entry into the tall Traffic Type cab is a little more awkward from the rear than from the front so the rear hinged doors on the later Traffic Types did have their advantage in ease of entry.

By shortening the truck's nose, the new design resulted in 3ft shorter overall length and a 5ft narrower turning radius than a comparable conventional truck. It did, however, retain the same load platform length. The shorter overall length had another benefit on Traffic Type tractor models where the load shift to the front wheels allowed for increased fifth wheel load capacity.

As mentioned, Mack introduced its Traffic Type in two models, the CH with a 3-5-ton capacity and the CJ with a 3-1/2-6-ton capacity. Not coincidentally, the CH corresponded to the conventional BM and the CJ to the BX. As would be expected of trucks with differing load capacities, the engine power rating varied between the two models: the CH's engine was rated at 106hp and the CJ's at 117hp. The engines on both trucks could be exposed by removing the forward scuttle and floorboards. For major overhaul or replacement, the engine was removed from the front of the truck, which, of course, required dismounting the radiator. To help reduce the engine's overall height, an updraft carburetor was used. Other mechanical features of these trucks included vacu-

In 1933, Mack introduced a new line of "pug nosed" Traffic Types whose shorter turning radius made for easier maneuvering in tight inner city streets and alleys. Distinc-tive features of these early Traffic Type models included a large two-piece windshield and set-back doors.

um-actuated four-wheel brakes and Mack's dual re-duction rear axle.

The original Traffic Type design had a pro-nounced European look, similar to Fiat as well as Leyland trucks of the period. In 1936, Mack re-designed its Traffic Types for a completely flat front and the rear hinged doors mentioned previously. Now the line included not just the CH and CJ, but also several E models, which extended Mack's Traf-fic Type offerings into the lighter-duty range. The new EC model, for example, offered a load capacity from 1-1/2-3-tons. Although E and C Series Traffic Types look identical, close inspection reveals an easi-ly recognizable appearance difference.

Even though once the appearance difference be-tween the E and C Series Traffic Types is pointed out it is readily visible, one almost has to see the trucks side by side to make the distinction. This is because the difference is in the placement and height of the grille, even though the grille shape is nearly identical on trucks from both series. On an E Traffic Type model the grille is positioned lower and has a crank hole in the bottom. On a C Traffic Type the grille is mounted higher on the front of the truck and the crank hole is below the grille. If Mack's designers thought it necessary to make an appearance difference between their Traffic Type models, they certainly did it in a nearly invisible way.

Besides the new flat-front styling, a major change in the new Traffic Types over the earlier models is in the method by which the engine is extracted from the truck. On the newer C and E Traffic Types, the engine mounts on a sliding frame member that can be pulled out through the front of the cab once the grille and access panels are removed. The idea of a sliding engine platform is all the more ingenious when one realizes that with the engine located inside the cab—the "doghouse" on this Traffic Type design completely fills the center of the cab between the driver's and passenger seats—the only other way to remove the engine would be from the bottom and that would be a very tricky operation.

Although Mack's sales brochure for its restyled C Series Traffic Type describes the cab as commodious and comfortable, in reality a huge engine tunnel crowds the driver into a narrow alley on the left side of the cab. In addition to an engine that takes up the lion's share of the cab's interior space, the metal engine covers must have passed lots of noise into the cab. Fortunately for their drivers, most of these trucks were used for shorter hauls in urban areas with frequent pickup and delivery stops so the engine's din didn't have to be endured for hours at a time. Overall, the cab interior can best be described as spartan with only an array of instruments on a stamped sheet metal panel mounted in front of the steering wheel to compete with the road for the driver's attention.

As with Mack's other larger capacity gear-drive trucks, the Traffic Types transferred power to the drive wheels through a dual reduction rear end. Brakes were vacuum boosted. Common body types included an open stake platform or enclosed van, bottle truck, and tanker. Later Traffic Types with their flat-front cabs had a modern look that doesn't even appear dated more than a half-century after the last models were built.

In 1936, Mack redesigned its Traffic Types, giving the new trucks a flat nose and rear hinged doors. A very similarly styled truck also appeared in the E Series. The main difference between the C and C Series Traffic Types is seen in the location of the grille, which is higher on the C models.

Although production ceased on the CH and CJ models in 1941, Mack put its Traffic Type cab and chassis back into production in 1944 to build a run of 700 tractor models, called the NJU, for the U.S. Army. Mack Museum

Although production ceased on the CH and CJ models in 1941, Mack put the Traffic Type cab and chassis back into production in 1941 to build a run of 700 tractor models for the U.S. Army. Identified as the NJU, these military Traffic Types featured four-wheel drive. Other modifications for military use consisted of a more rugged channel-type bumper, which replaced the chromed-spring steel bumper on the civilian CJ and CH models, and stone guards mounted in front of the headlights and grille. Although a needless appurtenance for a military truck, the NJUs carried the Mack bulldog "leaping" out of

the truck's front above the grille. Somewhat humorously, the grille guard included a "shield" to protect the Bulldog in wartime's hostile environment.

After the war, Mack reintroduced the CJ and CH Traffic Types, with virtually no changes in appearance, as with the LMU and LJU.

With fewer than 1,300 CH and CJ Traffic Types built, these early cabovers cannot be considered one of Mack's successes, but they did provide Mack with a presence in a growing market, a market Mack would reenter with much greater success in the 1960s.

Chapter 9

Mack in World War II

The United States maintained a "hands-off" posture toward the European war that erupted with Germany's invasion of Poland on September 1, 1939, until President Roosevelt persuaded an isolationist Congress to pass the Lend Lease Act in March of 1941—ten months after the fall of France. However, many American manufacturers, including Mack, entered into contracts with Allied armies much earlier. In 1939, the French government placed an order for Mack model EXBX tank transporters that were delivered to British North African forces in 1940. (Between Mack's receipt of the order and its completion, France had surrendered, and rather than allow the trucks to fall into Nazi hands, they were shipped to Allied forces.)

The British also placed orders for tank transporters and other cargo trucks with Mack. Working with British military staff, Mack engineers developed the NR-4 tank transporter based on the newly introduced heavy-duty L Series, which were delivered under the conditions of Lend Lease. In addition, the British placed orders for hundreds of type EH, EHT (tractor), EHU (cabover), and EHUT (cabover tractor) trucks. The US military also turned to Mack for several models of trucks including 4x4 cabover tractors based on the CH and CJ. Apart from olive drab paint, a driving front axle, and brush guards for the grille and headlights, the military cabovers, identified as the NJU Series, differed little from their civilian counterparts. The Army also commissioned a purely military truck, the NO whose size and brawn would make it Mack's most notable World War II model.

With the December 7, 1941, attack on Pearl Harbor, Americans suddenly awoke to the realities of war. Yet years of isolationism had kept industry largely focused on civilian production and the military in a state of alarming unpreparedness. Shortly after issuing its declaration of war, Congress established the War Production Board. This board would act as a mega-corporation by coordinating the pro-

duction facilities of the entire nation as though all were part of a single manufacturing operation until the cessation of hostilities in 1945. Besides overseeing production, the War Production Board (WPA) had the important function of deciding which companies were best suited to manufacturing the many thousands of items of war materiel needed to fight a global war. New medium-duty tanks, the M-3 "Lee" and M-4 "Sherman" required heavy-duty transmissions. Mack's experience building strong heavy-duty transmissions led to its receiving a main order for this critical component. During the years of the war, Mack built 4,600 power trains for M-3 and M-4 heavy tanks. In another related order, Mack received contracts for crash truck bodies to be mounted on Brockway and Kenworth chassis. And the Mack bus plant in Allentown was converted to build Vultee aircraft for the Navy.

On February 10, 1942, Mack, along with the rest of America's automotive and truck building industries ceased production of civilian vehicles. What followed was the largest outflow of military production in the history of the world. By the height of the nation's war manufacturing effort, the automotive industry employed one million men and women who collectively produced $1 billion worth of armaments a month. So highly productive was American industry that by the June 6, 1944, Normandy invasion, 16 million tons of war materiel had been transported to England, along with 4,000 seacraft and 11,000 warplanes. America's enemies had predicted victory based on the long lead times needed by industries to tool up for war production; however, America's industries had converted to full war production in a matter of months. In the annals of history, American industry during World War II would become known as the "Arsenal of Democracy."

Mack played its part in the war effort by building 4,500 5-ton four-wheel trucks and 26,000 NO, NR six-wheel trucks. The four-wheel trucks had front

Mack's most famous wartime truck is the 7 1/2 ton NO, shown here pulling the Army's "Long Tom" 155 mm field gun. Note how the 6x6 NO dwarfs the 4x4 Jeep, hitched to a 37 mm anti-tank gun. Mack Museum

drive axles and were built in both truck and tractor configurations. The tractors saw use towing pontoon semitrailers while the straight trucks were equipped with van bodies to house and transport Signal Corps equipment, supplies, and various field equipment. The typical truck configuration used a 163-1/2in wheelbase, had a GVW rating of 27,300lb, and was powered with Mack's 529ci engine.

The six-wheel trucks were 6-ton 6x6in general purpose heavy-duty vehicles designed for transporting heavy loads and towing heavy artillery and other nonmotorized equipment. These trucks were fitted with both closed and open cabs and carried a cargo body. Specifications for these 6-ton 6x6s, which were also built by Brockway, Corbitt, and White in addition to Mack, called for a 177in wheelbase, 707ci engine, and a GVW rating of 35,960lb.

Mack's most famous wartime truck is the 6x6 NO, used as a prime mover rather than a cargo truck. By a "prime mover" the Army meant a truck that towed rather than carried. Most wartime photos of the NO show it pulling the Army's "Long Tom" 155mm field gun. It was also used to pull 8in howitzers. The NO was a 7-1/2-ton truck with a 156in wheelbase and overall length of 297in. Its Mack EY six-cylinder overhead-valve gasoline-fueled engine produced 170hp from a displacement of 707ci. The truck carried a fuel capacity of 160gal, which gave a range of 160miles.

The NO was one of the lowest geared trucks used by US forces in World War II. Top speed, full throttle, in first gear, low range nudged the speedometer needle only slightly past the 1mph peg. Top speed in fifth gear, high range was a not-too-nimble 31mph. From the five-speed transmission and two-speed transfer case power flowed to a dual reduction axle at the rear and a triple reduction axle at the front. The final gear ratio at each drive axle was 9.02:1.

As has so often been the case at Mack, the NO's front drive axle was an engineering wonder. Nearly all front drive designs have a weak "Achilles heel" in the universal joints used to transfer power to the front wheels. The front drive axles require universal joints to allow the wheels to angle through their turning radius. Mack eliminated universal joints from the NO's front drive axle by placing bevel gears on the top and bottom of each front wheel kingpin, then installing matching gears at the ends of each axle shaft, both on the longer shafts from the differential and on the short shafts holding the front

wheels. Seen stripped of its housing, the NO's front drive axle is a machinist's wonder, containing seven precision gearsets as well as ten sets of tapered roller bearings supporting the gears and shafts. By making the kingpins powered members of the front drive axle, the wheels could turn without distorting the power flow. Another advantage of eliminating universal joints was that all driveline elements were enclosed, dramatically reducing wear caused by mud and grit that get packed into exposed driveline parts as military trucks slog through roads better described as quagmires. No one ever accused Mack engineering of cutting corners—even to meet wartime production demands—and it's this unswerving dedication to ruggedness and reliability that has earned Mack its world-famous reputation: "Built like a Mack truck."

The description with this photo of a Mack NO serving in the European theater reads: "19 August, 1944: American field artillery unit with its gun in tow moves through small French town enroute to the outskirts of Brest."
Mack Museum

As was common with World War II military trucks, the NO had an open, canvas-covered cab and folding windshield. Quite commonly these trucks were fitted with a circular gun mount and a .50 or .30caliber machine gun. NO cargo bodies were oak wood construction covered with canvas stretched over a U-shaped top bow structure. Due to their size, the two spare tires and wheels were carried inside the cargo body. A front bumper-mounted 40,000lb Garwood PTO-driven winch allowed drivers to pull a stuck truck free to retrieve other mired vehicles. A 3-ton chain hoist assembly at the rear of truck enabled the driver to raise or lower the pintle and hitch for coupling or uncoupling field guns and other towed equipment. To help relieve the truck's brakes from having to exert full stopping power for both the truck and gun unit, field guns were equipped with

brakes that the driver could activate by a hand-operated control.

A brute by anyone's standards, the NO was a huge truck best compared to Mack's FCSW. A man of average height standing alongside the truck might be able to reach the door handle if he stood on tiptoes and stretched his arm fully over his head. Production of the NO extended from 1942 to 1943. A total of 2,503 of these Prime Movers were built. Today the opportunities of seeing a Mack military truck "in the flesh" are practically nonexistent. However, the Mack Museum, located at the Mack factory in Allentown, Pennsylvania, has a meticulously detailed NO model in its display. This model may be the closest that any of today's Mack enthusiasts ever come to Mack's most famous wartime truck.

Mack developed the 6x4 NR-9 for British forces fighting in the Near East. Special features of this truck included a wide-spread bogie for mounting the high flotation tires needed for desert use. NR Series trucks were later used in Europe and served in the famous Red Ball Express that supplied the American Third Army, commanded by the legendary General George S. Patton, in its race across France and into the heart of Germany. Mack Museum

The NO's front drive axle was an engineering wonder. Nearly all front drive designs have a weak "Achilles heel" in the universal joints used to transfer power to the front wheels. Mack eliminated universal joints by placing bevel gears on the top and bottom of each front wheel kingpin then installing matching gears at the ends of each axle shaft and the short shafts to the front wheels. Seen stripped of its housing, the NO's front drive axle is a machinist's wonder—containing 7 precision gear sets as well as 10 sets of tapered roller bearings supporting the gears and shafts. Mack Museum

Chapter 10

L Series Heavy Haulers

As the 1930s drew to a close, Mack recognized a need to introduce a new truck line with heavier-duty ratings than the E models to replace the aging chain gang AC as well as the AP and some remaining B models. The result was the handsome L Series, which first appeared in 1940 and lasted until the mid-1950s, with some specialized L models being built into the 1960s.

Distinguishing features of the L line include a well-proportioned, split windshield, a massive grille similar to that used on the A and B Series, cycle-style front fenders, and tall side door windows.

Built in truck (LF), tractor (LFT), and six-wheel (LFSW) versions, the LF model became one of Mack's most popular sellers.

Distinguishing features of the L line include a well-proportioned, split-windshield cab that had a distinctively modern look and a massive radiator grille that would also grace Mack trucks of the subsequent A and B Series. Front fenders on the new L models were the so-called "cycle" style, named for their arched crown and styled similarly not only to the front fenders used on Mack's E Series, but also to the front fender design of International's heavier-duty K line models. Probably the most noticeable appearance feature of Mack's L line is the large amount of glass; the tall, slightly V'd split windshield and equally tall side door windows, give excellent visibility. As would be expected of a Mack product, the L line's fresh styling heralded major engineering advances.

Those who did not directly experience the Great Depression might assume that America had regained economic vitality by 1940 and the eve of World War II. However, this impression does not square with history. Full economic health remained elusive until the postwar era. Although many of the L models were built with special jobs in mind, Mack recognized the need for trucks that would prove their worth and advertised its L models, particularly the versatile LF, as "thrifty" and of "proven utility value."

Built in truck (LF) , tractor (LFT), and six-wheel (LFSW) variations, the LF model became one of Mack's most popular sellers with 12,453 units built between 1940 and 1953. (No production occurred between 1942 and 1944 due to Mack's commitment of its truck facilities to the war effort.) Although various displacement Thermodyne (overhead valve) engines were installed in the LF Series trucks, a popular choice was the EN 510 rated at 160hp. One of the unusual features of Mack Thermodyne engines is their use of two-piece cylinder heads. Both heads, each covering three cylinders, are identical and interchangeable. Transmission choices consisted of a five-speed or ten-speed duplex. Mack offered its duplex transmission either with monoshift or two shift levers. With monoshift, the operator worked only one lever and could select the transmission's dual range by flicking a selector under the gearshift knob.

True to Mack standards, even the LF was a beefy truck—built on a frame with channels 10-7/16in deep, a flange length of 3-1/4in and made of heat-treated, high carbon steel 7/32in thick. The LFT frame had a full 1/4in thickness. Brakes were hydraulic—tractor models had air-brakes—and all configurations featured Mack's famous dual reduction

Another popular L model, the LJ, could be ordered with diesel power.

rear axle. Suspension mounting points were rubber insulated, a patented Mack feature. Standard equipment included radiator shutters to control engine temperature. On the tractor models, a sleeper cab could be optioned, as could larger engines, auxiliary fuel tanks, and marker lights.

Moving up the model classifications, other popular L Series trucks included the LJ and LM, both designed for heavy hauling. Like the LF, the LJT and LMT tractor versions were also built. With its larger trucks Mack offered several diesels including the END405, 519, and 605. The LM line included an off-highway dumper designated the LMSW-M. This truck, developed in 1944, first saw use by the petroleum industry for hauling drilling machinery in the American Southwest. Later these trucks became a familiar sight in logging and mining operations. Distinguishing features of this model included military-style open fenders, offset cab, a double channel frame, and flat radiator similar to that used with the F and earlier B Series trucks. All LMSW-M trucks were equipped with power steering. The

LMSW-M tractor version had a GVW capacity of 100,000lb.

Having an even larger capacity yet, the LRSW was a six-wheel off-highway dump model introduced in the immediate postwar period and used in a variety of construction and mining settings. This massive truck, which was also built in single rear axle versions without the SW designation, shared many appearance characteristics with the LMSW, including military-type open fenders, an offset cab, and the flat radiator. Given this truck's tremendous load capability—115,000lb GVW or 180,000lb GCW—a pioneering planetary gearset was used in each drive wheel to achieve a sufficiently low gear reduction to move the enormous loads. Formerly, Mack used chain drive to obtain the power reduction needed for its super-duty trucks. The planetary gearsets, which Mack called Planidrive, also helped remove load strains from the shaft drive mechanism.

The Planidrive system was really quite simple and worked like this: Rather than driving the wheels

This LJT looks very comfortable coupled to its lowboy trailer.

Mack's L models worked in a wide range of settings. The truck shown here is equipped for heavy duty wrecker service.

Probably the most famous L model, the LTSW saw service in the "wide open spaces" of the American West. Although primarily used for multiple-unit freight hauling, *many like this example saw use in the logging industry— both on- and off-highway.*

directly, each axle shaft drove a sun gear around which three planetary gears revolved. The planetary gears walked inside a larger diameter ring gear, thereby effecting the great reduction in gearing. By using the Planidrive system, Mack was able to power a super-duty truck through substantially lighter axle and driveline components than would be required for direct gear drive without sacrificing strength and reliability.

Planetary gear reduction at each of the drive wheels was only one of the LRSW's innovative design features. Thanks to the superior flexing qualities of high-alloy springs, each wheelset could dip or rise to conform to terrain irregularities without transmit-

ting twisting stresses to the frame. At the same time, interaxle radius rods of massive size and strength assured perfect alignment of the axles and removed stresses from driveline components both straight going and on curves.

Mack engineers did not slight the LRSW's brake capability either, giving this truck not only extra large air chambers but also 1509sq-in of brake lining surface for tenacious and simultaneous braking action on all wheels. Two plungers from the air drive units activated the brake levers at each wheel. And, like virtually all Mack trucks since the 1920s, the LRSW surrounded the spring ends with massive rubber cushions to insulate the chassis from road shocks. To prevent side movement, massive "ears" on each side of the bogie preserved the frame's alignment in relationship to the rear wheels. No other super-duty truck of the era came close to matching Mack's engineering elegance, yet the LRSW's two most impressive engineering features, the Balanced Bogie and Power Divider, have yet to be mentioned.

By the Balanced Bogie, Mack meant equal traction, even tire loading, and uniform braking on all four—actually eight—wheels. While the suspension design and brake system already mentioned helped achieve even tire loading and uniform braking, the feature that set Mack six-wheel trucks apart from the competition and gave balanced traction between all both rear wheel sets, was the exclusive Power Divider—a device still covered under Mack patents and a unique feature of Mack trucks even today. The design and operation of the Power Divider has been discussed in some detail in the AK-AP chapter; however, some additional comments are also appropriate here.

Although Mack called the Power Divider a third differential, the device does not contain gears. Its primary purpose is to distribute torque in unequal proportions to the four drive wheels. Mack's service literature describes the Power Divider in this way: "It is not a friction device or a differential lock. It is simply a cam-and-plunger differential with a torque bias toward the side offering the greatest resistance." In operation, the Power Divider operates like this: under normal conditions it functions like a regular bevel-gear differential, providing equal torque to all drive wheels while allowing differences in speed between axles when the truck is turning. The Power Divider's distinctive torque-apportioning feature comes into play when the wheels on one side of the bogie lose traction. When this occurs, greater torque is directed to the wheels on the side still maintaining traction and the truck continues to move without bogging down.

It might seem that transferring torque to one set of wheels on a heavily loaded truck could put so much strain on the driveline that an axle might break. However, the Power Divider's design was such that it limited power transfer so that an axle would not break under the Power Divider's operation. Further, the Power Divider transmitted torque smoothly, without an abrupt surge that could cause wheels to spin or driveline parts to break.

The Power Divider also served another function as an interaxle differential. Unlike single rear axle trucks, six-wheelers—both those designed for on-highway as well as those designed for off-highway use—require an interaxle differential as well as the differentials in the axles to compensate for differences in travel between the two driving wheelsets of the bogie. Otherwise, when one axle encounters dif-

ferent surface terrain than the other, its wheels travel faster or slower to cover the same distance. Without an interaxle differential to compensate for this travel distance, driveline parts would bind up and shatter. On six-wheeler Mack trucks used strictly over the road, ordinary bevel-gear differentials are typically used between the axles. But for off-road use, the Power Divider with its torque distributing feature is unmatched in six-wheel operation.

Reflecting the frame's crucial role as a support structure for the body, drivetrain, and chassis, the LRSW's frame is made from extremely rugged alloy steel I beams with cross-members and mounting brackets electrically welded in place. From bumper

The LTSW's most striking feature is its hood, which seems long enough to cover two engines in tandem. This LTLSW (the second L standing for "light") can be seen at the Mack Museum.

to bogie, cab to chassis, the LRSW exuded brute muscle. To enable the driver to handle this mighty machine, power steering and air clutch were standard equipment. As mentioned previously, what sheet metal the truck wore was strictly purposeful in design. Typically a mesh guard sat in front of the radiator to protect the cooling device from stones or debris thrown up by equipment in this super hauler's lead. The hood was a simple three-piece unit consisting of side panels with large openings that allowed air to pass over the engine. A large exhaust stack protruded through the hood's basically flat top.

Although it might seem that with the LRSW, Mack had reached a pinnacle in both muscle and en-

gineering, the L line included yet another model that, if not superior to the LRSW in brawn, made an impression like no other truck of its era. This model is the famed LTSW—also a six-wheeler—which Mack introduced in 1947 and sold only in certain western states. This restriction allowed trucks engaged in distance hauling to be built with longer wheelbases and more powerful engines to handle that area's mountainous terrain. Most LTSWs were operated in one of the three following configurations: as a tractor pulling a semitrailer, as a tractor pulling both a semi and full trailer, or as a truck pulling a full trailer. Although this model was designed primarily for long-distance multiple-unit freight hauling, LTSWs also

L model fire trucks are both popular and strikingly handsome.

L model fire apparatus could be equipped with either open or enclosed cabs.

saw use in the logging industry, both on and off highway.

The LTSW's most distinguishing and striking feature is its hood, which seems long enough to cover two engines set in tandem. In actuality, raising the hood was likely to reveal a Mack EN 707A Thermodyne engine. The Hall-Scott 400, a 1090ci gasoline engine rated at 290hp on gasoline and 306hp on butane, was available in the LTSW at extra cost. The ten-speed Mack Duplex was the most common transmission choice for these trucks.

Because vehicle weight affects payload weight, Mack also built a light-weight version of its special West Coast distance hauler, identified as the LTLSW (the second L standing for "light"). Over a ton of weight savings was achieved by extensive use of heat-treated aluminum alloy for chassis parts including the bogie support brackets, frame cross-members, wheels and hubs, as well the hood. Externally the LTLSW looked identical to its weightier cousin. Today one of the few surviving LTLSW examples

can be seen in the Mack Museum in Allentown, Pennsylvania.

At the very top of the series, Mack also built a modest production of LV and LY models. A special off-highway LRVSW, built in the 1950s, had a capacity of 34 tons. Because the postwar run of chain-drive FW and FT Macks used the L line's cab with half-doors, at quick glance it's possible to mistake one of these trucks for an L model. But if the half doors confuse the truck's identity the F model's chain drive is certainly a giveaway.

As with all civilian trucks, L Series production was discontinued from 1942 through late 1944. The smaller L models were replaced in the early 1950s by comparable B Series models while the larger L models, namely the LR and LV, continued in production until the early 1960s when the full B line was finally in place. With the L models Mack retained leadership in the heavy truck field, achieving sales in excess of 30,000 units for all models.

The L Series enabled Mack to retain leadership in the heavy truck field. The Series, which ran from 1940 to the mid-1950s, with no production during the war years of 1942-1944, can be counted a sales success with more than 30,000 units built.

Chapter 11

A and B Series: Mack's Postwar Medium-Duty Truck Lines

With new styling and upgraded engineering, the A Series appeared in the mid-1950s to help Mack celebrate its 50th anniversary as America's preeminent truck builder. Although the A Series adopted the E cab with few changes, the grille bore a strong resemblance to the heavy-duty L models, helping Mack establish a family resemblance between its medium and heavy-duty trucks. Actually,

Although the A model trucks used the E Series cab and cycle fender design, the massive grille gave the new medium duty line a distinctive look.

Saturday Evening Post *ad announcing the Golden Anniversary Macks.*

the more massive grille gave the new trucks a sturdy, all-work appearance. So thoroughly does the plain painted, upright grille lend an air of ruggedness that Mack was able to carry over the essential design into the B Series.

At the outset, the A Series consisted of four models: the A-20 rated at 17,000lb GVW and replacement for the EF; the A-30 rated at 21,000lb GVW and intended as replacement for the EG; the A-40 rated at 24,000lb GVW, replacing the popular EH; and the A-50 rated at 40,000lb to 45,000lb GVW replacing the AQ.

In 1951 and 1952 Mack added several new, larger capacity models to the A line. Increased distance freight hauling by motor truck had expanded the market for semitrailer tractors, leading Mack to offer a semi-tractor in the A Series. Definitely not in the same league as Mack's L Series semi-tractors, the A Series tractors fit well in the intercity hauling market. Tractors were offered in both the A-40 and A-50 lines. The A-50 semi-tractor models consisted of a gasoline-powered A-54T and a A-51T diesel. An A-54S six-wheel tractor was also offered.

Gasoline-fueled A Series trucks were fitted with Mack's Magnadyne six-cylinder L-head engines. Initially three sizes were built starting with the 291—a number referring to the engine's displacement in cubic inches—which Mack installed in the A-20 models; the 321, which came in the A-30; and the 377, which Mack used in the A-40. A 405 Magnadyne was also built for the A-40 and heavier-duty models. Diesel models used Mack's END 510—a 510ci engine with the Lanova-licensed combustion chamber—that had been introduced with much fanfare in the E Series. An overhead valve Thermodyne gasoline engine rated at 158hp as also available in the larger models. A ten-speed duplex transmission (five-speed plus auxiliary) would also be optioned on the heavier-duty A line trucks. This transmission could be outfitted either as a monoshift (one lever) or with dual levers.

With the passing of the E Series, Mack had been without a cabover model in its lighter-duty truck line. To fill that gap, in the fall of 1951, the EFU COE model now renamed the A-20U was put into production. Another larger cabover model, the A-52U was also built. Neither were big sellers.

As their appearance suggested, the A Series were transition models—giving Mack a slightly more modern-looking product while waiting for a new medium-duty truck line with engineering and styling that reflected the advances of the postwar era.

The A's successor, the completely restyled and reengineered B line appeared in the spring of 1953, just three years after the first A models had entered production. Actually, many elements of the B's design had been in the works for several years. As early as 1948, Mack's product engineering group had begun development of a new medium-duty truck that carried the M8 designation. Essential styling features—the split V'd windshield, the gracefully rounded cab roof, and similarly rounded door window openings—first emerged in that engineering study. Interestingly, there's more than a passing resemblance between the lines of the Mack B Series cab and the cab styling of Studebaker's R and E Series trucks and pickups. Yet as far as can be determined, both are independent designs—Mack's design was an in-house product, and Studebaker's was a Bob Bourke design from Raymond Loewy Associates. And, if there were to be any thoughts of collusion, it's clear that Mack staked out the territory that would be fulfilled by the B Series first.

While the original M8 bore little resemblance to the production B models except for the cab, evolutionary developments in the M8 study brought it increasingly close to the final B design. For instance, by 1949, the M8 had acquired the tall upright grille and wide fender fronts that would be characteristic of the production models. Still, refinements would occur in the final design, including headlights recessed or "frenched" into the spacers between the grille and front fenders, and a simpler grille design borrowed almost intact from the A Series. In the early '50s, one of the hottest car customizing "tricks" had been to recess the headlights into the fenders rather than having them protrude from the fronts of the fenders in a sort of bug-eyed appearance as was the practice at the factory. Mack very cleverly borrowed the customizer's inset headlight design and in doing so greatly improved the B Series trucks' frontal appearance. This so-called "frenched" headlight treatment got its name from the French origin of this styling gimmick.

Although the B models carried numerous engineering updates, as well as a handsome styling upgrade, the first trucks built in this series shared major mechanical components with their A Series predecessors, including the Mack Magnadyne L-head gasoline engine. Most B Series trucks, however, are fitted with Mack Thermodyne gasoline or diesel engines. A Thermodyne engine is easily distinguished from the earlier Magnadyne engine by virtue of overhead valves.

While the Mack name carried a nearly legendary reputation for ruggedness, it also spoke premium price. Long before the arrival of the B line, Mack had built up a loyal following whose replacement trucks had to wear the famous Bulldog radiator mascot. Besides this group, there were others who would buy a Mack if they could justify the costs. To help launch the new B Series, Mack developed advertising flyers aimed at this second group of would-be Mack owners. In large orange lettering, the brochure's front panel asked, "Are your hauling costs too high?" This question had a double meaning. One reason for high hauling costs could be the price of the trucks. But Mack had another meaning in mind—and the brochure's purpose was to drive that meaning home

A Series Macks were fitted as fire apparatus. However, because the A served as a transition model and saw a very short production run, you're not likely to see many examples like this one.

with truck buyers who might wander wistfully into a Mack dealership. The second meaning to high hauling costs had to do with a truck's longevity and performance, not its price. As the flyer pointed out, "The initial price difference between the best truck and the cheapest truck is only a small fraction of your investment—but the difference in performance and reliability is another story. A quality truck will always outwork and outlive a cheaper truck many times over. Even more, a quality truck will generally cost less in terms of operational expense, downtime and maintenance." The brochure made its point with the statement, also printed in bright orange, "Invest in quality—move up to Macks."

The logic in this sales approach was sound and may have helped make the B Series Mack's best-sell-ing truck line to date. The idea of moving up to a Mack not only acknowledged the fact that most B models commanded a premium price over other makes of trucks, but also that Mack stood at the top of the heap, the best. And most everyone knows that when you buy the best, you get what you pay for. Plus, of course, a company operating the best equipment gives the appearance of being a well-run, profitable organization. In addition to these enticements, the flyer enumerated eight other benefits of owning a Mack truck:

• In the long run Mack trucks cost less to own and operate.

• Alone among truck manufacturers, Mack makes all its own major components incorporating dozens of unique, superior engineering features.

Introduced in the spring of 1953, Mack's new B line carried the latest styling features, including headlights "frenched" into the leading edge of the front fenders and a new cab whose rounded lines bore more than a passing resemblance to Studebaker's R Series trucks.

• Service records prove that Macks perform better, require less maintenance and downtime, and deliver more ton-miles per dollar.

• With Macks on the job, standby trucks are not needed—Macks are the best and cheapest insurance against breakdowns.

• Macks shrug off the toughest hauling jobs and come back for more.

• Fewer Macks are needed to accomplish the work of a greater number of less powerful and efficient trucks—also bringing savings in man hours of operation, fuel, maintenance, and insurance.

• Macks have greater value at trade-in time. The higher initial cost is repaid in the higher resale value, and most important,

• Mack takes complete responsibility for its products.

These were not idle claims. The B line proved equal to every claim the flyer made—and then some.

The B line consisted of a wide range of models, many of which were built in both straight truck and highway tractor configurations. At the bottom of the

Mack's B line spanned a wide range of models. One of the longest production models in this Series, the B-42, proved popular as a highway tractor. A 1962 example is seen here.

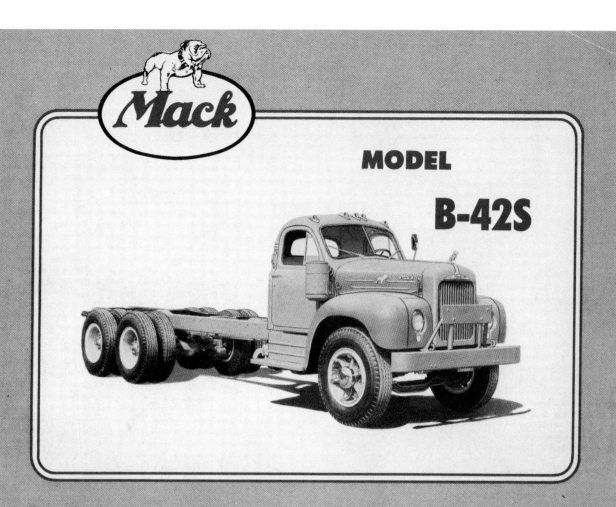

MODEL

B-42S

MODERN in design and construction, Mack B-42S six-wheeler, is a welcomed new-comer to dumper, mixer and heavy cargo operations. It is conceded to be the ideal six-wheeler on which to mount the newly designed load-forward mixers. This unit offers maximum capacity with compactness. By skillful engineering it is built to meet the challenge of increased-power-to-weight trend.

Standout features which when combined result in unequalled performance with lowest maintenance costs, include the new EN 401 Magnadyne engine of 150 BHP at moderate RPM. Engine reliability with matchless economy are advantages reflecting profit to the owner.

Further modernization is achieved by a new combination chassis frame and inside channel reinforcement, both of alloy steel and heat-treated. By use of such identical material both members inherently carry their correct proportions of the load. Exceptionally stiff cross-members of special design have been positioned to best meet the rigors of such severe service.

Front and rear ends have been specifically engineered for excessive load ability. New drop-forged I-beam front axles equipped with tapered king pin and thrust button which assures longer life and easy steering, are available to take full advantage of heavier front axle loadings permitted by certain States. A new lighter built but stronger four-wheel-drive Mack Bogie with exclusive Power Divider, is furnished. Banjos are of enormous stiffness and axle shafts alloy steel, graduated heat-treated for remarkable endurance. Balanced construction assures equal traction, even tire loading and uniform braking.

Driver satisfaction being of paramount importance, the new sturdy De Luxe cab features adjustable seats, unobstructed visibility, controls conveniently located and full driver protection, thus making driving safer, easier and more efficient. Wider front axle and shorter turning radius results in improved maneuverability.

Ad for Mack Model B-42S.

line were the B-20 rated at 17,000lb GVW, powered initially by the 290 Magnadyne engine, and the B-30 with a 211,000lb GVW rating, which was also available as the B-30T tractor model.

A key player in the B lineup from 1953 when this series was introduced was a B-42, offered in four- and a six-wheeler versions with load ratings of 40,000 to 60,000lb. While the B-42 proved popular as a chassis for mounting dumpers, mixers, and other heavy cargo bodies, it was also built as a semitrailer tractor. A B-42SW (six-wheel) model was also offered in both truck and tractor forms. By the time the B line was discontinued in 1965, sales totals would show the B-42 to be this series' second best selling model—with 19,729 B-42s built. As a representative B model, let's take a closer look at the B-42's features.

In standard form the B-42 consisted of a 170-1/2in wheelbase with a platform length of 144in. Optional wheelbases for straight models included 182-1/2in, 194-1/2in, and 222-1/2in providing platform lengths of 168in, 194in, and 240in respectively. The standard engine on early models was the EN 401 Magnadyne six-cylinder that produced 150hp from 401ci of displacement. The standard electrical system was 6 volts, with a 12 volt system listed as optional equipment. A five-speed TR 771 transmission was supplied standard equipment ; Mack's TRD 773 and TRD 7730 ten-speed duplex, monoshift transmissions as well as the TRD 77, TRD 770, and TRDX 770 ten-speed two-lever duplex transmissions were available at extra cost. The standard front axle carried an 8,000lb load rating while an 11,000l. rated front axle could be specified as optional equipment. On the standard wheelbase model, the alloy steel, heat-treated frame was constructed with one I beam and three channel-type cross-members. On the longer wheelbases, additional channel-type cross-members were added. For additional frame strength, buyers could also specify 1/4in fishplate reinforcing at extra cost. The 22gal standard fuel tank could be replaced by single or dual 40gal saddle tanks.

While early B models continued to use the L-head Magnadyne gasoline engine, most B Series trucks are fitted with Mack Thermodyne engines, either gasoline or diesel.

In 1956, Mack expanded the B Series with several new models in the heavier duty range. These trucks, which were intended as replacements for the LTL and LTLSW, used the older L Series cab. A 1964 B-75 six-wheel tractor is shown here.

Standard chassis equipment consisted of a channel-type front bumper, two combination stop and taillights, I.C.C. marker lights, electric horn, tool kit, tow hooks front and rear, left side rearview mirror, and a two-cylinder, 7-1/4cu-ft air compressor. Chassis color choices included Mack green, red, yellow, or blue. The extra cost chassis equipment list added automatic radiator shutters, radiator guard, 17,000BTU hot water heater with defrosters, air horn, and underframe tire carrier on 222-1/2in wheelbase models.

Moving up the series, the B-53 consisted of a weight saver dumper/mixer chassis powered by the END 673 diesel. In 1956 Mack expanded the B line with several new models in the heavier-duty range. These included the B-72, B-73, and B-75,

which were intended as replacements for the LTL and LTLSW, trucks designed to operate in the great expanses of the American West. To fit these new B Series models to the requirements of western trucking, Mack made extensive use of light weight alloys to maximize the haulage capacity. As an alternative to Mack engines, trucks in this Great Western Group—as the B-70 Series models were designated—could also be equipped with rugged Cummins diesel powerplants.

As mentioned previously, some of the early B Series trucks were fitted with the EN 401 Magnadyne gasoline engine carried over from the A Series. However, the Thermodyne overhead valve gasoline engine in several sizes and power ratings soon replaced the older L-head engine. By 1959, buyers were opting for diesel engines in a ratio of 3:1, and in 1962 Mack introduced its END 864 V-8 diesel, built in the Hagerstown, Maryland, plant. Over-the-road truckers trying to meet a delivery schedule delighted in this engine, which with its 255hp (without turbocharging) had the power to haul maximum legal loads at top highway speeds.

Along with new truck models and upgraded engines, Mack engineers also kept busy during the mid-1950s designing new transmissions. As alternatives to the base five-speed B Series models could be fitted with Mack's Unishift ten-speed, so named because a single lever was used to select all ten forward gears. Beyond the ten-speed, Mack also offered a Triplex fifteen-speed transmission and the Quadraplex twenty-speed gearbox.

In 1956, Mack also debuted its B-80 line of Super-Duty trucks designed as replacements for the LJ and LM models in the construction, mining, logging, and other off-road work. These flagship models are set apart from the rest of the B Series not just in size but also in the extreme ruggedness of their design. An exposed, cast tank radiator boosted engine cooling capacity while angular military-style front fenders not only gave the B-80 models an off-road look, but also resisted battle scarring far better than the rounded "civilian" style fenders. To support the heavy payloads, B-80 models featured full-length double channel frames. These trucks were available in single or double drive axle configurations and could be specially fitted with front drive axles. Rear axles employed Mack's patented dual reduction differentials while the front drive axle used a special triple reduction differential. Load capacities of the B-80 models exceeded 60,000lb GVW. As would be expected of a super-duty truck, most B-80s were equipped with diesel engines.

Mack also used the B chassis for fire apparatus. These handsome trucks proved highly popular with sales in 1955 rising 25 percent over the previous year and increasing another 38 percent in 1956. B Series fire apparatus were built as pumpers with pump ratings of 500, 750, 1,000, and 1,250gpm; and as hook and ladders with aerial ladders in 65, 75, 85, and

In keeping with their use for distance hauling, the B-70 Series tractors are often equipped with sleeper cabs. A 1958 B-77 model seen here.

The B-80 models are easily recognized by the larger, exposed cast tank radiator and angular, military-style fenders.

100ft lengths; and as straight trucks or in tractor and semitrailer configurations.

Due to the B Series long, thirteen-year production run, these trucks came to be widely recognized. Their shapely styling distinguished the B models from any other medium-duty truck on the road—a Mack's identity has never depended on someone's recognizing the bulldog leaping from the radiator crown or the Mack name and bulldog emblem on the sides of the hood. Strong product identiy is important. If a manufacturer's product looks like everything else on the market, how is that product going to develop its reputation with customers and the public. Perhaps for that reason, Mack has always

given its products something that's called "corporate identity."

The B line established its Mack heritage through the bold, upright radiator grille—nearly a direct carryover from the A models and also reminiscent of the L and even the F Series. To look right, the nose of a big truck needs a massive look, and that's what the upright grille did for the B models. Around and behind the grille, the truck flowed in graceful curves, giving the B Series Mack its timeless beauty. Yet attractive and appealing as these trucks are today, they were almost an anachronism when they appeared in 1953. Light truck styling, led by Ford's new F Series, were already advancing beyond the so-called "fat

B Series fire apparatus share the handsome profile that distinguishes this line.

Mack's B fire apparatus proved highly popular with sales showing a 25 percent increase in 1955 and rising another 38 percent in 1956.

Ad showing the range of B models.

fendered" styling school. The new F models that appeared in 1953 reflected a more angular look that
Chevrolet would adopt in 1955. Of course, there's
nothing that says big trucks have to look up to date.
V-ed windshields had been around since the 1930s,
so Mack wasn't breaking new ground with the split
windshield of its B models. However, the larger
glass expanse of the B cab over the smaller one-piece
windshield found in the A and E Series trucks was
sure to be appreciated by drivers.

The rounded cab, which bears more than a passing resemblance to International's D and K Series
models, first introduced in 1936, as well as Studebaker's R models introduced in 1949, was also an
anachronism when it appeared in 1953. But here too,
Mack's decision to adopt a familiar, if not advanced,
look paid off. There's something cozy, comfortable,
and timeless about the look of a B Series Mack—like
a pair of old slippers, a favorite chair, or a worn base-
ball glove. Around 1976, a friend purchased a B Series Mack to use in his log home business. When he
showed me his "new" truck, I had no idea as to its

vintage. It could have been a year or two old—it
looked that well cared for—or ten years. Nothing
about the truck's appearance gave away its age. I
think Jay remarked that his truck was an early 1960s
model, but its date-of-birth didn't matter. It was a
Mack, which meant that it would do all Jay asked of
it—and more—for probably as long as he needed its
service, and it looked downright handsome in a
rugged sort of way.

Besides appearance, the B Series cab offered several improvements over the former A and E Series.
First, and most noticeable, the V-ed windshield gave
better visibility. The instrument panel with the
tachometer centered in front of the driver and located above a similarly sized and shaped speedometer,
put these two primary gauges in easy view. Handy
for truck operators, the tachometer contained an
odometer-like counter for keeping track of engine
hours while the mileage odomoter occupied a similar place in the speedometer. Smaller round gauges
recording fuel level, engine oil pressure, coolant temperature, and brake air pressure flanked the larger

central gauges, two on the left and two on the right. For symmetry's sake, the glove box door on the right side of the cab matched the instrument panel's shape, including the rounded extension in the center that held the glove box knob.

No one would call the dash of a B Series Mack fancy, but it is pleasantly utilitarian. The A Series used a simpler gauge layout, placing the instruments in two ground housings: one for the speedometer and the other for the gauges. To eliminate the nightmare of troubleshooting gauge problems by lying on one's back on the floor of the truck, the B Series instrument cluster is demountable from the dash—a very helpful and thoughtful design. An ashtray sits between the gauge cluster and the glove box. As is expected in heavy-duty trucks, the interior is spartan: seat upholstery is durable naugehyde; door coverings are stamped metal panels; and the floor covering is a rubber mat. The most prominent items in a Mack B Series cockpit are the giant steering wheel

With its 13-year production run and several decades more of strong, faithful service, the B Series Mack has become the most widely admired and collected postwar truck.

Mack built 47,459 B-61 models, making this 1964 B-61 tandem dump one of the most popular B Series trucks.

The cast radiator was also used on some of the larger B-70 Series trucks.

and the shift levers, which straddle the cab's center section. The B Series cab is climbed into either from a running board or from a step set into the saddle-mounted fuel tank.

While the B Series production run, which lasted thirteen years, fell far short of the 22-year production span of both legendary early Macks, the AB and AC, the total of all models in the B Series accounted for the largest production total of any Mack series to date. In all, Mack built over 127,000 B Series trucks—a number that's the equivalent in big truck circles to a gold record for a recording artist. When the replacement R models arrived, Mack offered a B and C to R conversion kit to update the out-of-production B and C models. The update kit consisted of an R cab

and hood/front fender assembly ready to install on the B or C chassis. Unless the cab had become worn, the upgrade made little sense because the B Series never really fell out of favor.

While the modern and distinctive R line continued to be a strong seller, the timeless looking B Series models have a charm that the newer trucks lack. Today, B Series Macks are a favorite with collectors, rivaled only by the early chain gang trucks. And why not, a B Series Mack looks every bit as handsome and serviceable in the 1990s as it did when it debuted more than forty years ago.

Now that B Series Macks have been out of production for nearly thirty years, there are enough parts around from scrapped and otherwise derelict

IT TAKES MORE THAN A BULLDOG

TO MAKE A Mack

Why does this youngster sport a Mack Bulldog
on his toy truck? For the same reason that
many drivers of other makes fasten the Mack
Bulldog on their trucks.

A man can dream, can't he? It's natural to want
the best; but neither the man nor the boy is
fooling himself.

They both know that it takes lots more than
a Bulldog to make a Mack.

Economy-minded truck owners know it too!

3092

IT'S PART OF THE LANGUAGE . . . BUILT LIKE A MACK

"It takes more than a Bulldog to make a Mack."

Two of the most notable Mack models, the AC on the left and B model on the right. Today, only the "chain gang" AC surpasses the B model in collector interest.

trucks not only to help collectors preserve restorable models, but also to enable craftsmen and customizers to have some fun. In recent years I have seen two examples of Mack lovers creating eye-catching pickups using B Series cabs and forward sheet metal. One of these "Baby Mack" pickups appeared at the Mack Museum in Macungie, Pennsylvania, on a bright sunny August day while I was poring through the museum's archives doing research for this book. The truck's owner came inside to describe his creation to Mack Museum curator Colin Chisholm. Colin beckoned to me as he followed the owner out to inspect the truck. This "Baby Mack" sat on a late model Chevy pickup chassis. Painted bright red and lavishly adorned with chrome, this rugged looking hauler was a sight to behold.

There's at least one other "Baby B Series Mack" that has appeared in recent years with the Antique Truck Historical Society (ATHS) display at the Antique Automobile Club of America's (AACA) fall meet in Hershey, Pennsylvania. If Mack had decided to build a light truck in the postwar years, most likely it would have looked like this Baby B model. George Sprowl, Sr., who operates a trucking business in Searsmont, Maine, created his "Baby Mack" from a junked 1956 B30 and a burned out 1983 Ford F350. To fit the Mack cab to the Ford pickup frame, George narrowed the cab five inches and channeled it over the frame three inches. Scaling the B Series front fenders down to pickup truck proportions required more complex metal working. Likewise, the hood and radiator grille needed sectioning to match the pickup's narrower width and lower height. To

A Mack enthusiast constructed this Baby B model Mack by fitting a B cab and front sheet metal to a 3/4 ton Chevrolet pickup chassis. That's Colin Chisholm, curator of the Mack Museum, admiring the truck.

give the truck a Mack feel, Sprowl replaced the F350's coil springs with Mack air ride suspension and installed a 105hp Cummins 4BT diesel. Sprowl noticed that Dodge pickup rear fenders blended well with the rounded B Series lines, so the truck carries a Utiline (stepside style) Dodge pickup box and fenders. So that those approaching the truck from the rear will recognize what they're seeing, the tailgate wears M-A-C-K lettering.

It would be fun to listen in on the reactions these trucks create as they drive down the highway.

"Hey, lookit. What kinda pickup is that?"

"It says Mack, and wow, there's a bulldog on the radiator."

"Mack didn't build pickups; they make big trucks."

"Well it says Mack."

"Boy, that's the truck I'd like to own."

As early as 1948, Mack's product engineering group began development of a new medium duty truck to replace
the E Series. Styling features that would come to charac-
terize the immensely popular B models—the split V-d

windshield, gracefully rounded cab roof, and similarly
rounded door window openings—first appeared in this
engineering study. Mack Museum

Chapter 12

Mack's Early-Modern Nonconventional Trucks: H, W, D, N, MB, F, G, and C Series

Although Mack's B Series proved to be adaptable to a wide range of weight classes and uses, it was a conventional design truck. To fill the market needs for nonconventional models, during the B line's production run Mack built several specialized truck models that can be grouped under the letter designations D, N, G, MB, F, and C—the order in which they were built. For the most part, the trucks built under these letter designations used the cabover design, which provides for a very short cab and engine space and allows for maximum cargo length. The cabover design also has the advantage of being highly maneuverable in tight areas and so is ideal for city use.

In Mack tradition, several new and innovative features appeared on these "interim" trucks, making them in several instances quite "nonconventional" indeed. What is also somewhat unusual is that the C models were actually built as the last trucks in this letter designation group, rather than the first, and will be presented in that order in this chapter. Production of trucks in this grouping was by no means as large as the popular B Series, but each filled a special slot in Mack's truck line. Another contrast with the B line, with the exception of the ungainly H models, the styling of the other models represented at least current, if not advanced truck design. What's more, most trucks from any of these series still look up to date today. Yet, their modern appearance also causes these trucks to lose their Mack distinctiveness. Apart from the Mack nameplate, typically positioned under the center of the windshield on the front of the cab, and the pouncing Bulldog found on some models in this grouping, the Mack identity might not even be noticed. For this reason, even though trucks in this letter grouping have the same vintage standing as B models, trucks from the B Series have a much higher standing with collectors. Of course B models are also more plentiful.

What's common between the B Series and the other nonconventional models built during the same period is their shared Mack ruggedness. The powerful, advanced engines developed during the B's production run were also used in the H, W, D, N, G, MB, F, and C models. Although overlap exists between many of the models in this letter grouping, each has its own distinctive styling and characteristics—a clear testimony to the creativeness of Mack's engineers and designers. We'll start first with the H Series.

As Mack's first completely reworked postwar cabover truck, the H Series achieved its purpose of allowing extra-long trailers, but it also had an ungainly appearance. The H models are easily recognized by an extremely tall cab that quickly earned this truck its "Cherry Picker" nickname. Appearance aside, a short bumper-to-back-of-the-cab length of under 10ft enabled H model tractors to pull long 35ft trailers and stay within the 45ft legal overall length limits enforced in many states. This long trailer capability, plus the use of Mack Thermodyne gasoline or diesel engines, made the H Series trucks popular for distance hauling. In 1954, Mack reworked the H cab, lowering its height by a full foot. These revised H models can also be recognized by the more bulbous front and vertical as well as horizontal grille. Simultaneously with the H cabovers, Mack released the W-71 model, designed specifically for the West Coast market. This truck is also characterized by a stub-nosed appearance.

For intercity service Mack developed still another line of cabover trucks, identified as the D Series. The first of these models appeared in the spring of 1955. The extreme forward location of the cab, which actually mounted ahead of the front axle, caused the engine to be positioned between the seats. A second unusual feature of this design in addition to its forward cab location is the manner by which access is made to the engine. Instead of hinging the cab so that it could be tilted forward for service, the designers located a "elevator mechanism" at the rear of the cab that raised the entire cab structure several feet above the chassis, exposing the engine and related mechanical parts to easy service. The mechanism for raising the cab came in two forms: one that used a mechanical jacking device and the other, which used a hydraulic ram. The hydraulic lifting mechanism was, of course, faster and easier to operate. For marketing purposes, Mack coined the term *Verti-Lift* to describe the elevating cab concept.

In 1953, Mack reestablished itself as a builder of nonconventional trucks with the H Series. The extremely tall cab led drivers to give Mack's H model the nickname "Cherry Picker."

The D cab has a European look with its sloping windshield but angular lines. The grille opening is a two-piece affair consisting of a wide upper section above a narrower lower section, which is flanked by the headlights and parking lamps. The grille and light supports attach to the chassis and remain in place when the cab is raised. Cycle-style fenders cover the front wheels, which are positioned behind the doors. Locating the cab at the very front of the chassis, ahead of the wheels, offered drivers excellent visibility and provided the short turning radius, which is so important to maneuvering in the tight confines of city delivery. Rather than cabover, a better description of these trucks is "cab forward." One reason for the cab's extreme forward position is that placing the seats ahead of the wheels allowed a lower cab profile than is possible with a true cabover design.

Two types of D models were built: a delivery truck that ranged in load ratings from 20,000lb to 28,000lb GVW, and a semitrailer tractor with load ratings ranging from 40,000lb to 53,000lb GVW. The D Series model identification scheme followed a pattern similar to that used in the B line with the D-20, D-30, D-42 P, D-40, and D-42.

The D models represented several advances, including power steering, which proved a real plus on a truck that put the engine's weight ahead of the front wheels. All models in the D Series offered Mack's Magnadyne gasoline engine as standard equipment. Although they were well designed for their specialized use, production of the D models was short lived, extending only to 1958—fewer than 1,000 units were built.

In 1958, Mack replaced the D models with another cab forward line identified by an N designation. The N group offered more models that were available in the D Series and produced somewhat higher sales, totaling slightly under 2,000 units. The most significant feature of the N models is their use of a Budd-built cab, which looks identical to the forward control tilt cab used on Ford C class trucks of the same period. The only external differences, apart from each manufacturer using its own emblems, is a slightly different grille. Beneath the skin, mechanical differences abound with Mack N models offering a wide range of Mack engines, both gasoline and diesel, as well as transmissions from five to twenty forward speeds. The Ford C class trucks used Ford engines.

Unlike the elevating feature found on the D models that raised the cab for servicing, on N models the cab tilted forward to give access to the engine and other power accessories. The tilting mechanism was very simple, but well designed. Two hinges on the front of the chassis frame served to secure the cab as well as allow it to tilt forward. At the rear, the cab was held in place by a locking mechanism that, when released, enabled an operator or service technician to easily tilt the cab forward. So that the cab wouldn't tilt too far forward and to reduce the amount of effort needed to raise the cab from a locked position, the tilting mechanism had a counterbalance spring that was compressed when the cab sat in locked position. Like the tension springs that assist in opening a garage door, this spring released tension as the hood was tilted forward until it reached a neutral point with the cab about halfway through its tilting arc. As the cab tilted forward from this position, the spring again came into tension. When the cab was pushed back into position on the chassis, the counterbalance spring's tension again

In 1954, Mack restyled the H Series cab, bringing the truck's overall height down a foot and pushing the grille slightly forward for a mildly "stub-nosed" look.

Simultaneous with the Model H's introduction, Mack introduced the W-71, a larger capacity cabover specially designed for West Coast use.

helped reduce the effort required to lift the cab.

Mack's N models carried load ratings of 28,000lb to 65,000lb GVW (N-42 through N-61) and were available with a wide range of engines—both gasoline and diesel—as well as five-, ten-, fifteen-, or twenty-speed transmissions. The N's biggest detractor was its very similar appearance to Ford's cabover trucks. In 1962, after a short four-year production run, Mack phased out the N models, replacing them with the MB Series. Slightly fewer than 2,000 N model trucks were built.

The MB is an interesting truck in that it combined features of the D models, particularly the grille styling, with other features of the N models, notably the tilt cab. The MB cab, which was a Mack design, differs from the D cab mainly through the use of a nearly vertical— rather than slanted—windshield. Like its D and N predecessors, the MB's cab forward design allowed a low overall cab height.

Designed as both a highway and city truck, the MB line included both semi-tractors and delivery trucks. Mack supplied these trucks with the six-cylinder END 475 diesel as standard equipment. This engine, which was built by Scania-Vabis, developed 140hp and featured a combustion chamber designed similarly to Mack diesels. For buyers wanting a gasoline-fueled engine, Mack also equipped MB models with Chrysler hemi-head V-8s, a rugged engine rated at 189hp. Trucks in the MB Series could be equipped with a variety of manual or automatic transmissions providing up to twenty forward gears and three reverse speeds when combined with inte-

grated high-low compound gearsets.

The MB is a no-frills truck with a cab interior that is every bit as spartan and businesslike as its exterior. The gauge panel consisted of a slanted, rectangular metal surface into which was set a smaller rectangular gauge cluster containing the speedometer/odometer, voltmeter, oil pressure gauge, and temperature and fuel gauges. The tachometer was placed a few inches to the right of this main gauge cluster and the air pressure gauge was positioned a few inches below the main cluster. The metal panel also held various controls including the key/starter switch, headlight switch, reserve air valve, auxiliary brake valve, engine stop button, throttle, and others. Also located on this panel were the cigar lighter and ash tray, plus warning plates listing governed engine speeds, shutdown instructions, and cold start procedures. An equally no-frills console between the driver and passenger seat held the cab heater and ventilating controls.

What the MB cab lacked in beauty it made up in functionality. With its large windshield area, the MB cab offered drivers an excellent view of the road. The main and compound transmission shift levers (on trucks so-equipped) were positioned beside the driver for ease of operation. Although most servicing was done from underneath the truck by tilting the cab forward, radiator coolant could be checked or topped by opening a door in the center of the Mack nameplate on the front of the cab.

Like Mack's previous trucks with the cab forward design, the MB's set-back front axle made it possible to mount full-size bodies on a shorter wheel base. For maneuverability in tight spaces, in combination with these trucks' reduced overall length, the front wheels were given a 45deg turning angle. Mack built the MB in various model configurations from 1963 to 1971. Slightly more than 2,000 were built.

In 1959, Mack introduced a line of super-short tractor models called the G Series. These trucks made extensive use of lightweight materials and were designed for West Coast operation. What is distinctive about these trucks is their extremely compact cabs and short bumper-to-back-of-cab (BBC) dimensions. The reason for designing a cab with a thickness little more than the width of the doors and perching this cab on top of the front wheels was to allow the longest possible semitrailer or full trailer and semitrailer combination, since trailer length was regulated by overall truck length. With the G models, Mack achieved an extremely compact BBC dimension of 51in 80in when a sleeper compartment was added.

To reduce weight, the cab was constructed of aluminum. Optional aluminum chassis components were available to reduce weight still further. With an over-the-road truck, savings in vehicle weight mean

For inter-city use, Mack developed the Model D, a more radically-designed truck with the cab actually positioned ahead of the front wheels. Locating the cab at the very front of the chassis offered drivers excellent visibility and provided a short turning radius which is so important to maneuvering in the tight confines of city delivery. Two types of D models were built: a delivery truck, shown here, and a semi-trailer tractor. Mack Museum

a heavier payload and greater profitability.

Although the G models were designed with a flat grille like the D, N, and MB Series, the windshield slanted back slightly and the cab corners were rounded for a modern look. In fact, the styling advances of the G models over their D predecessor are nothing short of remarkable. With their front fenders and awkwardly shaped cab design that almost looks home-built, the D models would appear to be a definite antique if seen on today's highways. A well-preserved or restored G model, in contrast, could easily be mistaken for a fresh-out-of-the-showroom truck. Besides appearance, the new design also made for greater ease of operation and maintenance, as well as added driver comfort.

In keeping with their mission of hauling large loads over extended distances, G models were offered with a variety of Mack and Cummins diesel engines—both turbocharged and naturally aspirated—with the most powerful turbocharged Cummins engine rated at 335hp. A manually operated hydraulic mechanism tilted the cab forward giving access to the engine and forward chassis components. Despite their advanced styling and engineering, the G models showed sluggish sales results, with slightly in excess of 2,000 units built over a three-year run. In 1962, the G models were discontinued, replaced by the upgraded and highly suc-

Offering a full range of advanced
Mack engines—gasoline, diesel, turbodiesel—

Two great new MACKS

New look in a proved performer

New! Compact! And with power to earn

One of the most unusual features of the model N, shown in the lower right, is that Ford also used the same cab on its late 1950s C class trucks.

The MB line, which included both semi-tractors and delivery trucks, combined the grille design of the D models with the tilt cab of the N models. What the MB lacked in beauty it made up in functionality. Its large windshield offered drivers an excellent view of the road while the tilt cab made for easy servicing. Radiator coolant could be checked or topped up by opening a door in the center of the Mack nameplate. Mack Museum

cessful F Series.

In standard form F Series trucks have an even shorter BBC dimension than the G models they replaced: 50in to 51in. Two sleeper cabs are available: the regular sleeper, which gives a 70in BBC dimension, and the deluxe sleeper, which stretches the bumper-to-back-of-cab length to 80in. Although introduced in 1962, the F Series are modern-looking trucks, even thirty years later, and are easily distinguished from the G models by their square grille opening, "panoramic" windshield that curves around to meet the set-back side pillars, and a visible seam around the roof stamping. This seam acts as a water gutter to prevent the driver from being soaked from rain water running off the roof when he rolls down the door window or opens the door. To help control heat buildup in the cab, Mack used heat resistant glass for the windshield.

Another significant feature of the F Series is the dramatically upgraded cab interior. Consoles containing heater controls as well as other knobs and gauges straddle the center of the cab, putting the driver in a sort of "command control" position over all the truck's functions and physically separating the

For West Coast operation Mack introduced a line of su-per-short tractor models called the G Series. These trucks made extensive use of light weight materials and featured *an extremely short bumper to back of cab length of only 51in.* Mack Museum

driver's area from the passenger side of the cab. On some F models, the instrument panel as well as the side consoles have an attractive wood-grain finish. The gauge clusters are arranged so that the principal

gauges and controls are located in front of the driver on three separate panels that are placed directly in front and to the left and right of the steering column. The panel directly in front of the driver holds the

Although first introduced in 1962, Mack's F model still has a modern look. Besides styling, the F models also benefited from a dramatically upgraded cab interior and a wide range of diesel engines. Mack Museum

tachometer and speedometer/odometer as well as the auxiliary brake warning light. The left-hand panel contains a warning light that monitors engine coolant level and oil pressure, plus gauges showing engine oil pressure and coolant temperature, and a voltmeter that shows battery condition when the starting switch is "on" but the engine has not been started as well as charging rate when the engine is running at operating speeds. The right-hand panel contains the air pressure and fuel supply gauges as well as switches for operating electric windows, switching the clearance lights on or off, controlling the panel lights, turning the headlights on or off, and starting the engine. All gauges are round and highly legible with white lettering on a black background and with white needles and black bezels.

Fresh air ventilation to the cab is provided by a roof vent. The vent hatch is designed so that it can be

The C Series Mack used existing parts to create a conventional-looking truck with a bumper-to-back-of-cab dimension of only 89in.

raised with the opening facing forward or toward the rear. In bad weather, or to "air out" the cab, the vent raised so that the opening faces toward the rear of the truck. For fresh air ventilation, the vent is raised with the opening facing forward. The vent hatch is located directly behind the clearance lights at the cab's forward brow.

Like the MB Series, the cab on F model trucks tilts forward for service. In the earlier models, the cab could be tilted to a 42deg angle. Later models allowed a full 90deg forward tilt for better engine accessibility. The earlier tilt mechanism used torsion bars to counterbalance cab weight whereas the final design controlled cab tilt with two hydraulic cylinder, each of which incorporated a safety mechanism that locked up the hydraulic cylinders if the cab began to move too rapidly in either direction.

Mack supplied the F Series with a variety of engines, including the END673E, a 672ci displacement six-cylinder diesel rated at 180hp; the ENDT673, a turbocharged version of the same engine rated at

225hp; the ENDT673C, an even stronger version of this engine rated at 250hp; the ENDT675, an engine with very similar specifications to the ENDT673, rated at 235hp; the ENDT865, an eight-cylinder diesel displacing 866ci and rated at 325hp; the ENDDT865, a stronger version of the ENDT865 rated at 285hp, and the ENDT866, an engine with specifications similar to the ENDT865, rated at 375hp; the Super250, a 927ci six-cylinder diesel rated at 250hp; the NHC250, anther 250hp, six-cylinder diesel; three NTC engines—the 290, the 335, and the 350—all six-cylinder diesels displacing 855ci with horsepower ratings matching the engine numbers; the NTA370, a similar engine rated at 370hp; the V903, an eight-cylinder diesel displacing 903ci and rated at 320hp; and the 8V71N, also an eight-cylinder diesel, displacing 568ci and rated at 318hp.

It is common to see F Series tractors in six-wheel configurations. Long 54in front springs provided an improved ride over the short BBC tractors offered by competitors. This, and the truck's many superlative

One of the C model's more unusual features is the hinged
fenders that swing forward for access to the engine.

features, made F models very popular with over-the-road truckers, substantially boosting Mack sales. In 1966, Mack introduced the FL-700 Series built exclusively at the Hayward, California, plant. This line, which was designed for western operators, featured a slightly restyled version of the F Series cab and made extensive use of weight-saving aluminum, which allowed greater payloads.

To further expand its market penetration, in 1963 Mack introduced its C line—an interestingly designed tractor series that combined a conventional cab and set-back engine with a stubby hood to achieve a BBC dimension of only 89in with a conventional-looking truck. Flanking the short, sloping hood, which measured only 3ft in length, were fenders from the truly conventional B models. Since the short hood made engine access difficult, the fenders were hinged at the front so that they could be unbolted from their rear attaching points and swung around the front of the truck. Swinging the fenders forward exposed the wheels and side of the engine, which could now be accessed easily just by lifting the hood. Support rods kept the fenders from bending when they were unbolted from their attaching points.

What is most clever about the C Series is that Mack created this new truck line from existing parts—and did so with a BBC dimension that allowed the stub-nosed tractors to pull 40ft trailers—and stayed within the 50ft tractor/trailer overall length. To enable the C Series tractors to pull extra-size loads, the END864 V-8 diesel engine, rated at 225hp without turbocharging, was listed in the engine options. Despite its several beneficial features, the C Series lasted only two years with slightly more than 1,500 units built. Its replacement was the U Series (an R line derivative) discussed in the next chapter.

The decade from the mid-'50s to mid-'60s was a busy one for Mack's design engineers, particularly those assigned to developing new nonconventional truck models. The trucks that appeared during this period represented the principles of successful manufacturing: (1) fill as many market niches as possible, and (2) continue to refine your product. Some, like the C models, represented a design experiment that would be fulfilled more satisfactorily by later, more refined designs. Others, like the F, were highly successful and remained in production for many years. Maybe because nonconventional trucks are so purely functional, or perhaps because the nonconventional design seems synonymous with modern trucks, these nonconventional models are big favorites with collectors, though certainly not as popular as the conventional B Series trucks built during the same period. Those who buy and restore older Macks, either for hobby or business, show preference to models on which the Mack identity has been etched—and that never quite happened to these early-modern nonconventional trucks.

Chapter 13

Mack Enters the Modern Era:
R, U, and DM Series

By the 1960s, the B models were looking out of date. The time had come for Mack to step forward with a replacement line that matched the B line's distinctiveness as well as match or surpass the B's reputation for durability. One of the ways a company maintains its leadership position is by creating products of distinction. Mack clearly faced this challenge in designing and engineering its R Series' truck line.

The new series needed stand-out styling that the public would identify with the Mack name. It wasn't enough to create a truck that would be accepted by the trucking industry. Mack had a larger reputation to uphold with the general public. The slogan "Built like a Mack truck" had become a common expression, used by anyone to describe the integrity of virtually any object. It was important that the new R Series be different enough from every other truck on the market that anyone—whether buyer or bystander—having once seen the Mack name over the truck's grille, would forever recognize an R model as a Mack product. And, of course, the new trucks had to meet Mack's legendary reputation for ruggedness. The designers and engineers did their job well. Although different than the former B Series models, the R models are original when compared to all other trucks (except for the Brockway Husky which also used the R cab), and their performance has warranted the Mack name.

The R line entered production in 1965 so that early models of the new trucks could be seen on dealer's lots alongside the last B models, which were finally phased out in 1966. Since the R models represented an upgrade for Mack's conventional cab trucks, the popular cabover F Series and MB nonconventional city delivery trucks remained without change. Among the R Series more distinctive features is the one-piece fiberglass hood and fender assembly that is front hinged and tilts forward for servicing the engine and front chassis parts. Two latches that attach to the cab near the end of the front fender opening hold the hood assembly in place when it is closed. Tilting the hood and fender unit is a simple maneuver, requiring only that the latches on both sides of the cab be unfastened. Then, grasping the Bulldog and using it as a handle, anyone can easily angle the hood assembly forward.

Unquestionably the most distinguishable feature of the R Series is the tall cab with its high, nearly vertical windshield. Although the R cab looks larger and offers considerably more headroom, its width is actually the same as the B Series Flagship cab. Thanks to the squared-off vertical lines of the grille and high hood, the tall cab doesn't look at all out of place and helps give the R models their distinctively Mack look. The high windshield also provides a link with another popular Mack series, the L line trucks of the 1940s that were also distinguished by their tall cab and high, nearly vertical windshield. As would be expected, the high windshield and large side windows provide drivers of these trucks with excellent forward and side visibility.

The R cab also adds to the driver's comfort with a fully adjustable chair-height seat and increased use of sound deadening insulating materials—particularly in the more current models. Besides the cowl vents, the R Series cab is equipped with a roof vent that is opened by moving a lever recessed into the roof of the cab. The roof vent can be opened so that it scoops air from the front of the truck for a ram-ventilation effect or so the opening faces the rear of the truck in order to duct air out of the cab. Two air scoops located between the marker lights, help to direct a strong ventilation draft into the cab when the roof vent is opened in forward position. The rear opening position is used in inclement weather and allows a good ventilation through the fresh air vent with the windows closed.

Instrumentation consists of easily readable round gauges with the speedometer side by side

Mack R Model Equipment Hauler 1965-Present

1965 Model R equipment hauler.

with the tachometer, which is on the left, rather than vertically stacked as was the case with the B models. All instruments are grouped in an oval-shaped, hooded cluster located directly in front of the driver and use white needles and lettering on black background for high legibility. The throttle control, light switches, air starter valve, stop engine switch, and other knobs and levers are located to the right of the instrument panel and at the front of the dash above the heater unit. The key starter switch is located on the front of the dash, immediately to the left of the steering column.

The R line, which remains in production in the 1990s, consists of models from 26,000lb GVW grouped in three number series (the R-400, R-600, and R-700) and fitted with a range of gasoline and diesel engines in both inline six-cylinder and V-8 configurations. The earliest R models could be fit-

ted with engines with power ratings ranging from 140hp to 255hp. In late 1966, Mack made a significant breakthrough in diesel engine development with the introduction of its Maxidyne "constant horsepower" engine. By limiting the engine's fuel intake as rpm increase, engineers were able to control turbocharger boost thereby leveling the horsepower curve. The result was an engine that developed its maximum hp from 1,200 to its maximum governed engine speed of 2100rpm. The broader horsepower range reduced driver effort and transmission wear by eliminating frequent shifts and helped keep the engine from lugging on grades. Fuel savings also resulted.

To familiarize drivers with the differences in power characteristics between the Maxidyne and conventional diesel engines, Mack's R Series Operation Manual gave these instructions:

"With the Maxidyne diesel engine, it is not necessary to keep the tachometer needle "against the pin." This engine develops high horsepower between 1200rpm and governed rpm of 2100. Actually, the developed horsepower is 206 at 1200rpm, 235 at 2100rpm, with a peak horsepower of 237 at 1700rpm. The substantially constant horsepower of this engine permits the driver to maintain the highest possible road speed with a minimum amount of gear shifting, as no downshifting is required until the tachometer approaches 1200rpm. This allows the engine to operate at its peak horsepower, which is also its best economy range. Perhaps the biggest surprise that a driver will experience, in comparing this with conventional diesel engines, is the feel of increased power at lower engine rpm and wide open throttle."

To match the Maxidyne engine's ability to deliver maximum horsepower over an extended rpm range, Mack developed a new five-speed "Maxi-torque" transmission that featured a very short case design and lightweight construction. To keep drivers unfamiliar with the Maxidyne engine's constant horsepower characteristics from shifting at too high an rpm and overspeeding the engine, the Operation Manual cautioned drivers to allow more time on upshifts to let the engine fall into the shifting range of 1200 to 1300rpm. A clutch brake, which the driver engages by releasing the clutch then moving the shift lever through detent to neutral and again depressing the clutch through the last 1in of travel, can be used to slow the transmission countershafts thereby allowing shifts to be made more quickly.

In 1970, Mack introduced a higher powered Maxidyne diesel with a maximum horsepower of 325 as well as additional Maxitorque transmissions beyond the five-speed developed earlier. The new transmissions included a five-speed and overgear, Duplex ten-speed, Triplex fifteen-speed, and

The most distinguishing characteristic of the R Series is the tall cab with its high, nearly vertical windshield.

Here's something unique in trucks . . . the cab is offset to the left 11½" to give the driver better visibility ahead and behind for safer passing, backing and spotting. Short-coupling 90" BBC keeps driver low, allows tractor to haul longer trailers, permits more load up front and better load distribution. Yet there's ample room for any of Mack's full line of diesels, 180 to 375 hp with matching transmissions from 5 to 18 speeds. Wide front axle provides better turning angles and better stability. There's a large rear window to facilitate attaching trailer. A fiberglass tilt hood and fenders offer quick accessibility to the engine. The air cleaner induction pipe is isolated from the cab to cut interior noise levels. Excellent heating and defrosting systems.

The offset cab makes sure there's no mistaking a U Series truck. Moving the cab eleven inches to the right made for excellent visibility.

Quadraplex twenty-speed. Mack also continued to offer conventional-design transmissions that were often ordered on heavy-duty models, as well as a six-speed automatic transmission. At this time, Mack also introduced a refined "Dynatard" engine-compression brake system—one of many mechanical improvements that has kept the R Series up to date into the 1990s

As early as 1946, Mack had designed high-powered, lightweight trucks specially suited to the mountainous travel and great distances of the western states. To develop an R Series western model, Mack established an engineering task force dedicated to this purpose at Allentown in the spring of 1965. The task force had the simultaneous assignment of developing a West Coast model of the F Series COE (cab over engine) trucks. The group worked swiftly, finishing two prototypes by November 19 of that year. Mack Western was given charge of the new West Coast models, both of which were built in the Mack Western's Haywood, California, plant. The FL entered production first in 1966, with the RL following in 1967. The L in the series designation stood for light, indicating the weight-saving material used in these trucks' design. Both the FL and RL models featured aluminum frames and other optional lightweight components.

While an RL can't be easily detected from its standard R counterpart, there's no mistaking the U Series trucks that also use the R hood, fenders, and cab, but place the cab in an offset location. The cab was moved 11in to the right, which made it look like someone either chopped off the right portion of a wide cab or positioned a normal cab incorrectly on the chassis, but there was reason behind the designer's seeming "madness." Although unique to modern trucks, the offset cab had a history at Mack; the design had been widely used on the off-highway trucks the company had built post-World War II. With trucks, practicality often overshadows aesthetics, and Mack's engineers had a practical reason for mounting the U Series cab in line with the left fender—improved driver visibility.

Mack intended the U Series, which it described as an "unconventional conventional type tractor," as a replacement for the C Series that was phased out in 1965—the same year the U models were introduced. Like the C line, which also combined features of conventional style and unconventional design trucks to give a short 89in BBC dimension, the U tractors also had a BBC dimension of just 90in. With their well-conceived, if unorthodox, design, the U line models were an instant success and have continued in their popularity as is evidenced by the number of these distinctive trucks that can be seen plying the nation's highways.

Apart from the unusual cab location, Mack did little to distinguish the U and R models. Both used

Mack designed its DM Series trucks for the rugged conditions of the construction industry. The Series letters stand for Dumper/Mixer, the most common equipment application installed on this chassis.

the same engines and transmissions and had identical cab appointments as well as front hood and fenders. The major difference—the offset cab—had to do with the difference in intended use for the two lines of trucks. In its R Series, Mack offered straight models as well as tractors, whereas the U Series consisted only of tractors. Although semi-tractor drivers become very adept at maneuvering long trailers using only the rearview mirrors for a guide, when they sit in line with the left side of the truck, as is the case with a U model, drivers get an even greater sense of command over the truck they are piloting. This positioning allows a glance backward along the trailer to

affix its location when maneuvering into a terminal loading dock.

By adapting the basic R/U platform in yet another direction in early 1966, Mack created its DM Series platform for trucks exposed to the rugged conditions of the construction industry. The series letters stood for Dumper/Mixer, the most common equipment applications installed on this chassis, although platform bodies were also fitted. DM model trucks used the offset U line's cab due to the benefits in visibility and maneuverability realized by placing the driver at the truck's outer left side. Aside from cab location, all other features of the Command Cab, designed initially for the R Series—including the large glass expanse for excellent visibility and convenient placement of controls and gauges—can be found on U and DM Series trucks.

While the smaller DM-400 and DM-600 models used the fiberglass tilt hood and fender assembly of the R and U Series, the larger DM-800 models were equipped with a unique steel, butterfly-type hood and flat, squared-off, steel front fenders. To service the engine in trucks with this hood design, the hood sides can be unlatched and folded up accordion style as had been the practice on conventional model Mack trucks through the B Series. To get at more of the engine than would be accessible by just raising the hood, the front fenders were designed and mounted so that they could be easily unfastened from the cab and tilted forward. DM-400 and 600 model trucks used in construction settings where the more vulnerable fiberglass hood and fender assemblies would be easily damaged were often ordered with the steel hood and front fenders—as were R models used in similar settings.

To give its dumper/mixer-type trucks the low-speed power needed for hauling heavy loads on rough, off-road terrain, Mack offered the TRDXL1071 Maxitorque LO-LO transmission. While very similar in design and using the same main case as the TRL107 five-speed Maxitorque, the LO-LO transmission added a compound gearset that provided a low range gearing in first and reverse. The LO-LO range is restricted for nonhighway use only because the 24.55:1 low-forward gear reduction (low-reverse gives a reduction ratio of 25.20:1) places a severe strain on drivelines and rear axle gears above crawling speed.

Following a practice Mack had adopted in the 1930s of relating model numbers to weight capacity, the DM Series included the following model designations: DM-400/600, 43,000 to 66,000lbs; DM-600SX, 66,000 to 76,000lbs; DM-800, 66,000 to 100,000lbs. To give the DM-800 models better weight distribution, the front axle has a greater set-back on the chassis relative to the front of the truck than is the case in the smaller DM models. Although the DM Series originally offered only trucks with 6x4 drive configurations, in 1967 6x6 all-wheel-drive and 8x6 triple-axle drive became available.

Toward the end of the socially turbulent '60s, Mack introduced a "stars and stripes" paint scheme that became popular with those using its trucks in construction settings where "hard hat" workers had become symbolic of the nation's patriotic "silent majority." Although Mack had long represented American qualities of hard work and integrity, this was the company's only attempt to make an openly political statement through its trucks.

The DM Series has enjoyed the same long production life as the R and U Series from which it is derived. Like pace-setting Mack models of earlier eras, notably the AB and AC, the distinctive cab design and continuously updated mechanical components have given the R, U, and DM Series a production span stretching from the mid-1960s into the 1990s.

Chapter 14

Brockway Huskie

In August 1956, Mack Trucks signed an agreement with Brockway Motor Company of Cortland, New York, that led to the acquisition of a truck builder whose heritage and reputation rivaled Mack's.

Trucks with the Brockway name could be traced to 1910. Unlike Mack, which built chain-drive trucks into the postwar 1940s, Brockway had adopted Hotchkiss shaft drive on all its truck models by 1917.

Although Mack acquired Brockway Motor Co. as a wholly owned subsidiary in 1956, trucks with the Brockway name could be traced to 1912. The Mack Museum displays two Brockway trucks built prior to Mack's takeover—a 1946 model powered by a Continental 42BX engine and a 1910 Brockway "MotorWagon" powered by an unusual three-cylinder, two-cycle engine that is air-cooled.

Although no single Brockway ever achieved the fame of the AB or AC Mack, Brockway trucks gained a loyal following. An odd page in the Brockway history book was its lack of diesel-powered models. Although specializing in heavy-duty trucks, Brockway's engineers distrusted diesel engines and waited until the early 1950s to offer diesel power. What makes this fact even more strange is that in 1928 Brockway had merged with Indiana Trucks, which had been using Cummins diesel engines since 1931.

As might be expected, one of the first changes Brockway buyers noticed after the Mack purchase was the availability of diesel engines—primarily Cummins and GM. At the time of the purchase, the Brockway line consisted of twenty models, ranging from 20,000 to 65,000lb GVW ratings. Apart from the interference over diesel engines, Mack's management allowed Brockway to operate it as an autonomous company using the staff that had been in place before Mack's acquisition. At first, this approach worked well. Although Brockway's share of the heavy truck market had never been large, the Brockway division was highly profitable in the early years of its alliance with Mack.

In 1958, Brockway introduced its Huskie model, some Mack influence can be seen in the selection of the Huskie mascot—a stylized Alaskan sled dog perched on the crest of the radiator, a not-too-subtle imitation of the world-famous Mack bulldog. Although the Huskie was built in tractor, cargo, and tandem-axle models, sales of the Brockway nameplate amounted to only 10 percent of Mack's sales.

In 1961, the Huskie line expanded to include new medium- and medium-heavy-duty models with a short bumper-to-back-of-cab (BBC) dimension of only 90in. The new models consisted of cargo trucks, which ranged in GVW rating from 23,000 to 36,000lb, tandem axle models ranging in GVW from 40,000 to 50,000lb, and tractors ranging in GVW rating from 45,000 to 60,000lb. Engine choices included a 478ci Brockway-built overhead-valve six-cylinder gasoline powerplant rated at 200hp as well as lesser powered gasoline engines from Continental and the Cummins C-160 diesel, also a six-cylinder OHV engine rated at 160hp. Identified as the 158 Series, the new short BBC Huskie models wore a redesigned cab that differed from the earlier Husky models in its short hood, set-back front axle, and all-new cab that was distinguished by its all-metal, bolted construction and single-piece flat windshield. A novel feature of the 158 Series Huskies was that the front fenders at-

In 1958, Brockway introduced its Huskie line. Mack influence can be seen in the selection of the Huskie mascot—a stylized Alaskan sled dog perched on the crest of the radiator. Mack Museum

tached with just two bolts—allowing easy removal for engine service and maintenance.

In 1962, Brockway celebrated its 50th anniversary by plating the Huskie radiator mascot in 14 karat gold. The company's ads proclaimed, "It's the year of the...GOLDEN HUSKIE!...most advanced...most complete line in Brockway's history." Effective as the Huskie models had been in giving Brockway a line of modern competitive trucks, a large gap remained in Brockway's truck lineup—the absence of cab-over-engine models. In 1963, Brockway finally positioned itself as a player in the growing market for tall-cab trucks. The new 400 Series— Brockway's first cabover models—used the Mack F Series cab with a slightly modified painted grille that contained three horizontal bars and the Brockway nameplate. The 400 Series models continued Brock-

way's strong reliance on Continental engines— which had powered its trucks since 1913—but it also offered engines from Cummins and Detroit Diesel. Competitive though the new 400 Series models were, their addition to the Brockway line did not cause any significant increase in sales. In fact, they probably sowed the seeds of Brockway's ultimate demise as the company shifted from building "market niche" trucks to competing head to head with Mack.

In 1965, new 300 Series models with short 90in BBC dimensions that were similar in design to Mack's C Series, except for a different cab, joined the Huskie line. Brockway pitched the new 300 models to those preferring a conventional-style truck, but needing the extra load length as well as the maneuverability and excellent visibility offered by a COE. The short BBC dimension enabled the 300 models to

With its 400 Series, introduced in 1963, Brockway positioned itself as a player in the growing market for tall-cab trucks. Behind the Brockway nameplate, the Mack F Series cab is easily recognizable. Mack Museum

With its extremely short BBC length of only 90in, Brockway marketed its 300 models to those preferring a conventional-style truck, but needing the extra load length, as well as the maneuverability and visibility, of a COE. Mack Museum

closely match a COE tractor's load length at the same time it elevated the 300's cab by mounting it on an 8in substructure, which placed the driver at the same eye-level height as his counterpart in a 400 Series COE. This taller cab on a conventional truck made the 300 models somewhat unique and provided their much-touted "superior road visibility and maneuverability." The raised cab also gave the advantage of making room for larger engines. The 300 Series, which included single and tandem axle tractors, ranged in load rating from 23,000lb GVW to 73,000lb GVW on wheelbases from 130in to 217in.

Brockway continued its expansion in 1967 with the introduction of a 360 model that featured a redesigned cab and the option of either a conventionally located or set-back front axle. The set-back axle gave better load distribution on tractors hauling long, heavy cargoes.

The 360 Series with its choice of Cummins, Detroit Diesel, or Caterpillar diesel engines gave Brockway the strongest range of engine options the company had ever offered. To reflect this achievement, Brockway ads began proclaiming, "The most rugged truck in America Built by Brockway" and "In 1928 the most rugged truck in the world was a Brockway. It still is." Someone at Mack should have called foul when the second ad occurred. Top tough truck in 1928 a Brockway? How could a shaft-drive truck, powered by a four-cylinder engine compare in ruggedness with a six-cylinder, chain-driven AC or super-rugged AP Mack! These trucks weren't even in the same league.

The problem wasn't just Brockway's ad claims. Its new truck models paralleled Mack so closely that whatever market share Brockway gained came at least partially at the expense of the parent company. In 1975, Brockway introduced its new 700 Series, a line of high horsepower models that used Mack's R Series cab. Despite the similarity in appearance, the 700 models weren't Macks with Brockway name-plates—yet both competed for the same market. Oddly, the closer Brockway came to Mack, the more the Mack subsidiary lost ground. Despite having the widest range of models of its 61-year history, Brockway's profits had vanished and the company was operating at a loss. A proud company that had built its reputation with regional carries had set its sights on outshining Mack. The declining sales and profits that resulted would soon doom the company whose name—while not having the familiar ring of "Mack"—had stood synonymous with "heavy truck" for many, particularly in the northeastern United States.

As sales declined, Mack sought buyers for its Brockway subsidiary. At first, the prospects of a sale that would allow Brockway to continue under new ownership looked bright. On April 20, 1977, Steven J. Romer, a New York attorney and president of So-largen Electronics, Ltd., a manufacturer of electric cars, signed a purchase agreement with Mack for the Brockway name, manufacturing facilities, inventory, equipment, and dealer system. Romer claimed his interest in buying Brockway was because he had driven a Brockway truck on his first job after World War II and the experience had given him great respect for Brockway products.

The deal looked sure. Although Mack had been seeking $40 million for Brockway, the intent agreement signed with Romer reduced Brockway's price to slightly over $20 million. Besides continuing Brockway, Solargen also announced plans to build its electric cars in the Cortland, New York, Brockway factory. Prospects of the sale and new electric car business brought great relief to the Brockway work force who had been out of work since Mack closed the Brockway plant on Feb. 9, 1977, after 300 members of UAW Local 68 went on strike. Mack denied any connection between the strike and the plant closing, but surely the workers' walkout hastened Mack's determination to terminate a losing operation.

Hope for revival of the Brockway name and continuation of jobs at the Brockway plant quickly

Brockway's 300 Series included single and tandem axle tractors. Besides added visibility, the raised cab allowed space for larger engines. Mack Museum

turned to gloom, however, as financial backing for the purchase failed to materialize. With Brockway's permanent closing went a well-regarded name in the heavy truck industry. Though 500 employees of the Brockway plant in Cortland, New York, lost their jobs, Brockway truck owners continued to receive parts and service support from Mack branches and distributors after Mack Parts Division took over warehousing and distribution of Brockway parts. Mack also honored warrantees on recently purchased Brockway trucks through its area distributors.

Brockway's demise can be traced to numerous problems associated with operating a low-volume truck manufacturer and were unrelated to the wildcat strike on the eve of negotiations of the failed sale. Brockway's manufacturing facilities were dated and needed expensive upgrading, which did not serve

the interest of the parent company. Further, as early as 1974, the Brockway plant had been beset with labor troubles. Add to this the shortage of engines, increased governmental regulations including the anti-skid braking laws (MVSS 121), curtailed production, and depressed truck sales resulting from the 1973 recession—all of which caused Mack to take a hard look at the odds for Brockway's continued survival. The company's employees were among the best paid in Cortland, New York, and many of the jobs lost were irreplaceable. As one Brockway executive put it, "It is not a desirable situation for a smaller truck company to be owned by a larger one. You are always in competition with the parent firm and know they are going to take care of themselves first. Everything is fine as long as you're making money, but when you slip, watch out! You're part of a company, but really don't belong." That statement says it all.

In 1982, a company named J. Thomas Ltd. bought out the remaining stock of Brockway parts with the intention of providing parts service for the remaining members of the now legendary Brockway fleet. The company's four principal founders had all been former Brockway employees in various production, metal fabrication, and machining functions. Though none had management experience, they knew Brockway trucks and shared a dedication to keep the trucks alive. Along with the remaining Brockway parts stock, Mack consigned to J. Thomas Ltd. rights to manufacture any Brockway parts—but not the rights to use the Brockway name. So if Brockway is ever to be revived, it will either be at the hands of Mack or a company Mack designates. And with the Brockway name now dead nearly twenty years, its revival is unlikely.

Brockway's sales problems compounded when its high-horsepower 700 models took on not only a close Mack look, but also competed for the same market. The closer Brockway came to Mack, more sales ground it lost. Mack Museum

Chapter 15

Mack Trucks Today

The Mack legend stems from doing things right for nearly a century. But lately the going has been rough. In recent years the heavy truck industry, especially Mack, has been beset with tough financial times. Many truck enthusiasts may be surprised to learn that Mack Trucks—a trade name as American as Bandaid—is now a division of Renault, a French manufacturer.

In today's global society, however, the location of ownership has little bearing on the nature of the product. Today's Mack trucks are the best in styling, engineering, and stamina that the company has ever built. As evidence of this statement, the next time you're traveling an interstate, note the nameplates on the trucks on the road and watch especially for trucks with the Mack name and the famous Mack bulldog perched on the hood. You'll see lots of the venerable R Series rigs, but among the crop you'll also spot trucks from the current CH and CL Series. These sleek, high-powered conventional-style trucks are at the forefront of the industry in both engineering and design.

Features setting the CH and CL trucks apart from the older R models, as well as most of the competition's new models, include flush-mounted halogen headlights set into the forward edges of the front fenders and a massive, aerodynamic bumper that channels air up and around the cab for a slipstream effect. The smoothly sloping hood contributes to reducing the truck's wind resistance as does the mildly canted two-piece panoramic windshield.

On opening the cab door, one can readily see that Mack's designers have put driver comfort at a priority level equal to external styling and mechanical endurance. From the air-suspended driver's seat to the five-position, tilt/telescoping steering wheel to the highly visible instrumentation and luxurious interior color choices, these trucks reflect concern for enabling the driver to stay as keen and alert as

possible even after long hours at the wheel. Contrast the cockpit—a word which aptly describes a modern truck's control center—of a Mack CH/CL with a truck model as recent as a 1960s B; the difference is as striking as holding a simple, traditional screwdriver in one hand and a modern, electric-powered, cordless screwdriver in the other. Both tools can be used for the same task, but drive twenty screws with the traditional driver and you're likely to have blisters and aching wrists—not so with the power driver. The same holds true of today's Mack trucks where seating, visibility, location of the instrumentation and controls, and appearance of the cab surroundings all work together to reduce driver fatigue.

Always a priority at Mack, the construction and mechanics of the CH/CL trucks are world-class. Engine offerings span an array of diesel power in both six-cylinder and V-8 configurations, culminating with the 500hp Mack E9. Triple countershaft overdrive transmissions transmit power to bogies equipped with Mack's unique Power Divider. Power train controls use state of the art VMAC (vehicle management and control) electronics. Frames are heat-treated alloy steel and fitted with air-ride sus-

---

Mack Resources

Two major clubs encourage the restoration and preservation of Mack trucks:

The Antique Truck Club of America, Inc.
P.O. Box 291
Hershey, PA 17033

The American Truck Historical Society
P.O. Box 531168
Birmingham, AL 35253

At the top of the Mack lineup today are the CH/CL models. In comparison with the trucks shown earlier in this book, today's Ultraliners represent the very last word in driver luxury.

pension, making these trucks the smoothest hauling in Mack's history.

Trucks like the CH and CL give every evidence that the spirit of excellence that the Mack name has represented for nearly a century remains strong and alive. And this is as it should be if my grandchildren are to use the expression "built like a Mack truck" when they want to describe unsurpassed ruggedness.

Right
Today's Macks also offer world-class construction and mechanics, plus state-of-the-art VMAC electronics. Here's the modern CH600 from Mack's brochure.